STAR NAMES
for
BABY

The Origins
and Astrological
Implications
of All Common
(and Uncommon)
Names

STAR NAMES
—for—
BABY

The Origins and Astrological
Implications of All Common
(and Uncommon) Names

Dan Crawford

THE
DONNING COMPANY
PUBLISHERS
NORFOLK/VIRGINIA BEACH

To Joshua William Medina,
in none of whose names
I had any hand.

Copyright © 1989 by Dan Crawford

The Donning Company/Publishers
5659 Virginia Beach Boulevard
Norfolk, Virginia 23502

Library of Congress Cataloging-in-Publication Data:

Crawford, Dan.
  Star names for baby: the origins and astrological implications
of all common (and uncommon) names/by Dan Crawford.

  p.   cm.
  ISBN 0-89865-765-2 : $7.95
  1. Names, Personal—United States. 2. Astrology—Miscellanea.
I. Title.
CS2377.C73   1989   89-30300
929.4'4'0973—dc 19   CIP

Printed in the United States of America

CONTENTS

Introduction 7
How It Works 9
Aries 11
Taurus 25
Gemini 39
Cancer 51
Leo 63
Virgo 75
Libra 87
Scorpio 99
Sagittarius 113
Capricorn 127
Aquarius 141
Pisces 155

INTRODUCTION
OR
OH, BE STILL, MY BEATING HEART! ANOTHER BABY NAME BOOK!

If you are reading this in a bookstore, you can probably reach out and touch at least four other baby name books from where you're standing. What possible excuse can there be for bringing out another?

Well, in my experience, people who are naming a baby need all the help they can get. There's no reason for all this bother, of course. You, I know, would be courageous, name the tot Peter Cottontail, and have done with it. But not everyone has your strength of will.

I passed one of these mothers-to-be as she was checking her unborn's future in her astrological guide. Knowing how many baby name books she's shelled out for, I noted, "Pity there isn't a book that lists baby names by sun sign."

I was immediately sorry I'd said that, because I started to think about it. Astrology books list personal characteristics for those listed under the assorted sun signs; baby name books give name meanings that reflect personal characteristics. Why couldn't some book pair the names with the signs?

It should be made clear at the outset that this book will not pinpoint the single most nearly perfect name for your little bundle of bounce. The job's too important to leave to the stars alone. Suppose we went deep into the calculations and angles and proved that the only possible name for your infant is Juleida. But you hated your Aunt Juleida; she always kicked your kitten when she came over. There are some factors over which even the stars and I have no control.

My exceedingly unofficial research has, in fact, indicated that the most common consideration cited in choice of a name is a desire to avoid offending the relatives. This is just silly, because your relatives are going to be offended no matter what you do. That's what relatives are *for*.

What this book does is take over seven hundred common, garden-variety names and sort them by signs of the Zodiac. You get a lot of leeway here; if a name you like falls under the wrong sign, you can always modify it with a middle name taken from the proper chapter. The names are routine ones, with a few oddities tossed in because I thought they were pretty or because someone I owe money has kin named that. Double names like Rosemary, Daisy Jo, and Lulubelle have been weeded out. But keep them in mind; if some name doesn't quite please you, you can always tack on "belles" and "beths" until you like it. (Girls' names are particularly prone to these tack-ons; just about anything will sound like a girl's name if you add "ette" or "een.")

INTRODUCTION

The book has been kept to the basic lines of Peter, Paul, and Mary, and such names because, well, to be frank, folks who plan to name their darling Oprah or Elvis will do so for reasons of their own, and are unlikely to be swayed by the Zodiac. Much the same goes for people who insist on Maitreya or Bombazine. The sort of help these people need will not be found in this book. Try the Yellow Pages.

HOW IT WORKS

In each chapter, you will find something like this:

OPHIUCHUS
the Spoilsport
May 22 to August 21

The dates given for each sign are the generic ones you find in any astrological guide. They are as reliable as the weather forecast in your newspaper. Since the stars move around a lot—that's the point, after all—the actual beginning and ending dates for any given sun sign will vary depending on the year. In fact, any child born between the 17th and 24th may have been born under either the sign behind them or the sign ahead of them. Such people have three choices: They can (a) have a chart drawn up and find out exactly what the stars were doing at the moment of birth, (b) read the write-up for both signs and blend the characteristics into a personal profile, or (c) pick the write-up that sounds more flattering.

"Persons born under the sign of the Spoilsport are tall, have wavy hair, and have a tendency toward dimpled chins. They are often found on beaches—catching rays, or Zs, or both. Unless taken in hand early, they will grow up to be real estate developers."

Naturally, for the most accurate astrological profile possible, you have to go into a lot of factors besides the sun sign. Heredity and environment will make a difference to the personality, too. So if I say Ophiuchans are intelligent, it means that the general run of people born under that sign have something in their brain box. But there will still be Ophiuchans who don't know enough to pull their head in when they shut the window. The thing is that, if you're going to pick a name for the baby before it actually turns up, you aren't going to be able to take heredity, environment, and the more refined astrological calculations into account. These general guidelines are the best I can offer you.

"Semi-famous people born under this sign include Hatshepsut, Adeline Whiteoak, Hagar the Horrible, and Alfred E. Neumann."

I have tried to list someone besides the singers and statesmen who ornament most books of this nature. It will be noted by perceptive readers that a lot of these people became famous or semi-famous despite the fact that they didn't have names that go with their sign. Well, that's true. But who can predict, after all, what they might have accomplished had my wisdom been available when they were born?

(Say, if you aren't careful, your face will stick like that.)

Then you'll get a list that begins:

"SUGGESTED NAMES:

Tanith *(Anglo-Saxon)* *"What one doeth to leather"*

Since your Ophiuchus is likely to hang out at the beach, any name with Tan in it is a good bet. Related forms: Tanneth, Danith, Tannitz."

After each name, you see the linguistic origin in parentheses. You may ignore this. Onomasts, or name scientists, have been fighting for years about what language gave rise to this or that name. No one's sure yet, but we always put down our guesses so you know we've done our homework. I find, by the way, that hardly any of the authorities bother to specify which tribe of American Indian gave birth to the name, as though everyone from Nova Scotia to Chihuahua spoke the same language. But they are, after all, only onomasts.

"This name can also be used for Scorpio, Pisces, and Libra."

Most names will have these added loopholes, indicating that, yes, there are other possibilities available. For one thing, some names come in a variety of forms, some of which will fit one sign and not another, even though the meaning is the same. And, let's face it, name meanings are very similar all over because parents are very similar all over. They tend to lean toward names that mean "Great Wonderful Shining Star Who Is Fun at Parties." At least, I haven't yet run into a child named "Slightly Below Average, But Still Okay Once You Get to Know Him If You Don't Mind His Breath." The names meaning "God's Gift" alone would fill a book. So for a lot of names there is enough variety to allow for personal preference, and I have tried not to lock names too securely into a single sign. Remember that astrology makes a neat raincoat but a nasty straitjacket. (I read that in a Numerology book.)

ARIES
the Ram
March 22 to April 21

Aries is the first sign of the Zodiac, and nobody's surprised. Aries folks are the great competitors of the Zodiac. They *have* to be first, have to be winners.

They're built for the job, too, being brave, cheerful, hardheaded, and chock full of executive ability. Idealistic and generous, they have faith in themselves and in other people, brim with self-confidence, and are demonstrative in affection. They will never save a dime. If they need it, they always know where they can earn it or find someone to lend it to them.

Of course, there's always the other side. Arians are also naturally pushy, nosy, noisy, blunt, sarcastic, and reckless. The Arian is the typical business exec who slaps you on the back and shoves a cigar in your mouth, only to slit your throat a moment later because you stand between him and his profit. But that's just business, you'll hear as you bleed; nothing personal. Arians can't be bothered with personal grudges, even against themselves. A basic Aries will admit his sins and then run right out to commit them again.

With a short attention span and limitless energy, Arians have to be kept on a short leash if you want any kind of control at all. But Arians hate short leashes. Tell them it's good for them—they'll hate that, too.

Semi-famous Aries characters include Robert Bloch, James Branch Cabell, Bud Fisher, Jacques Futrelle, Linda Goodman, Hardie Gramatky, Henry Kuttner, Laura Jean Libbey, Sheldon Mayer, Melville Davisson Post, Leo Rosten, John Stanley, and Frank Stockton.

ARIES
GIRLS' NAMES

Antonia *(Latin) "Inestimable, beyond praise, priceless, super-nice, and all that sort of thing"*

That pretty well throws the cards on the table, doesn't it? This is obviously meant for Aries, Leo, and Scorpio, who do not generally lack for self-esteem. You may extend it to a Libra if you think people will exclaim, "Oh, she's precious!" The masculine form is Anthony, of course. Other forms for girls include Tonia, Toni, Antoinette, and Netta.

Anastasia *(Slavic/Greek) "Resurrection"*

You may apply this to Easter, which falls in this period more often than not, or you may refer to the rebirth of nature in spring, depending on your personal convictions. In either case it probably fits an Aries. Short forms of the name include Stacy and Tasia.

April *(Latin) "To open"*

The onomasts go nuts over this one, claiming it refers to the month when the ground opens for the growth of Spring. Others derive it from the Greek goddess of love, Aphrodite, though what that has to do with "open" I hesitate to guess. This is all for the experts to fight over, really. It is best for a child born in April, an Aries or a Taurus; you could extend it to Gemini, Leo, or Aquarius, who have open dispositions. Giving it to a kid born in December, though, is pushing it a bit. She'll be explaining it all her life. Male forms of the name are Avery and Averill.

Astrid *(Norse) "Divine strength"*

Aries is considered one of the strong signs, physically and emotionally. A real Aries will also gladly accept the alternate meaning, which is "impulsive in love."

ARIES

Bernice (Greek) "Brings victory"

Here is a wishful-thinking name for the warlike signs of Aries and Scorpio. Some people prefer the spelling Berenice, but no one knows how to pronounce that until they're told. Bunny and Veronica are considered forms of Bernice, but we are not convinced.

Bertha (German) "Bright, glorious"

This name obviously belongs to the spotlight-loving natives of Leo, Aries, and Scorpio. But I can hear you giggling about it even as I write this. Years of fat, jolly German Berthas in the funny papers have sort of tainted the name, and the Big Bertha, a massive piece of World War I heavy artillery, didn't help. "Bertha's Kitty Boutique" cannot alone offset the years of abuse. You can try one of the alternate spellings, Berta, Bertina, or Berthe. (This last should probably be pronounced "bairth" but you know everyone will say "birth.")

Brenda (Norse) "Sword, flame"

The experts can't agree on what language this is from, nor whether it means sword, flame, or both. Aries, being a warlike fire sign, can probably qualify for either. Brenda has been a very trendy name and will probably jaunt along as long as Brenda Starr is still running in the comics. It may be related to Brendan, or Brandon, or both, or neither. The onomasts haven't ruled on it yet.

Dawn (English) "Dawn"

Can't argue with that. Aries opens the year the way dawn opens the day. (Yes, we know the year starts in January. But day starts at midnight, too. I'd explain it all, but maybe you can take it from here on your own.) Oddly, the simple word "Dawn" is not enough for a lot of people, who came up with the variant forms Dawna, Dawnielle, and Dawnysia. There really are such people.

Donna (Latin) "Lady"

This is meant to imply the "lady of the house" that salesmen always ask to see, the woman in charge. The great boss signs of the Zodiac are

Leo, Aries, and Scorpio. Someone somewhere came up with the variant form Donella.

Ethel *(German) "Noble"*

This is another name for the egotists and leaders, Aries, Leo, and Scorpio. It is another name that has gotten a bad rap over the years. It just seems to sound funny to people, somehow. This is hardly fair to Ethel, but life is like that.

Florence *(Latin) "Flowering"*

This is another spring name, for Aries, Taurus, or Gemini. You might even extend it to Pisces, who shouldn't have to shiver back there in February without any consolation. There is no end to the variant forms for this name. The most common masculine version is Florian. Other feminine forms are Flora, Florida, Florette, Floris, Lore, Fleur, Fleurette, Flo, Florrie, Flossie, and, simply, Flower.

Gertrude *(German) "Spearwoman"*

The onomasts argue about some of the details of this name, but they agree a spear is involved somewhere. As such, it goes to the war signs, Aries and Scorpio. Like Ethel, Bertha, and a lot of the German warrior names, it is regarded as somewhat a silly name. No one has explained this or examined it in depth, as far as I know. There have been several famous Gertrudes, though, indicating it is possible to rise above such things. Variant forms include Gerta and Gertie, but the most popular one, achieving considerable independent existence, is Trudy.

Hilda *(German) "Warrior"*

Everything that went for Gertrude goes here as well. A variant form is Gilda, and some people claim Heidi as a form of it as well.

Janet *(Hebrew) "God's gracious gift"*

See John, under Aries boys, and Jane, among the Virgo girls, for details.

Kayla *(Hebrew)* *"Crown"*

The onomasts don't seem to like this name much, apparently feeling it is something some silly American parents made up. But others derive it from Kelilah, meaning "crown," which also gives us Kyle and Kele. Aries, Leo, and Scorpio will always believe they deserve crowns. It should be noted, however, that plenty of people still think this is just a fancy form of Kay.

Kitten *(English)* *"Kitten"*

That wasn't difficult, was it? The onomasts go all over showing how this is derived from Kathleen or Christine, or something, but there must be a few people who just want a plain Kitten. I took a lot of flak for tucking Kitten into Aries, too. Sentimentalists wanted it with the cuddly Libra names, and traditionalists wanted it with Leo, who is feline. You may do this, if you wish. But my experience with kittens brings to mind very earnest little creatures with great energy and abysmally sharp claws. Sounds like Aries to me. Believe it or not, there is a variant form of the name: Kitteen.

Lorna *(Latin)* *"Laurel"*

This is a form of Lawrence (see note) and, like it, goes to those people who always strive for the laurel wreath of victory, the Leos, the Arians, the Scorpios. Lorne and Loren are masculine forms, with Loren and Lauren sometimes going to girls.

Lucille *(Latin)* *"Light"*

This could go to any of the fire signs, Aries, Leo, and Sagittarius. Male forms include Luke and Lucius. Further female forms include Lucy, Lucia, Lucretia, Luz, Lucinda, and Lucilla.

Marcia *(Latin)* *"Warlike"*

This is the most common female form of Mark, and should go to the martial signs, Aries and Scorpio. It can be pronounced in two syllables (Marsha) or three (Mar-see-ya). Marsha and Marcie are variant forms.

ARIES

Matilda *(German)* *"Mighty in battle"*

This is another German war name, and goes to Aries and Scorpio. Like the other German war names, it is considered ludicrous and old-fashioned now, and, frankly, the variant forms don't help much: Matty, Tilda, Tilly, Mold, and Maude. Some onomasts feel that Maude or Maud was the original form of the name. Still, it may make a comeback with the Australian fad, these days. (I wonder if the Matilda Bay Cooler people would have paid me to say this name meant "mighty in bottle"? Too bad, another fortune down the drain.)

Myra *(Latin)* *"Wonderful"*

The experts seem to agree that this is not the feminine form of Myron, but a different name altogether. Obviously, Leo, Aries, and Scorpio are going to take the compliment to themselves. There are plenty of variant forms, including Mira, Mirabell, Myrena, Mireya, Mireille, and practically anything else the mind can come up with.

Myrtle *(Latin)* *"Myrtle"*

Myrtle leaves were used for a crown of victory and Myrtle is thus admirably suited to Leo, Aries, and Scorpio. Pet forms include Minnie and Mert, neither of which is considered especially glamorous.

Primrose *(Latin)* *"First rose"*

This is obviously a sign of spring and belongs to Aries. There may be some jokes about being "prim," but, frankly, not all that many people use the word any more.

Regina *(Latin)* *"Queen"*

This is another one of those royal names for Aries, Leo, and Scorpio. You could call her Reggie for short, but the accepted short form is Gina. Or do queens have nicknames?

ARIES

Renee *(French)* *"Reborn"*

Like Anastasia, this name can be applied to Easter or to spring, as you like. A variant form is Renata.

Robin *(English)* *"Robin"*

Yes, Mr. Onomast, I am aware that this name was really a male nickname for Robert when it started out. But there comes a time when you have to bypass the deep research and stay in the shallows. It is pretty firmly fixed in people's minds that this name refers to the red-breasted harbinger of spring, and what harm is there in that? Some people insist on Robyn or Robina. I suppose there's no real harm in that, either.

Rona *(German)* *"Mighty power"*

The onomasts are iffy on this, some of them thinking it's from the Gaelic for "seal," or just a form of Rowena. But the majority make it the feminine form of Ronald, a name of power and force. So it belongs in the Aries and Scorpio clan.

Roxanne *(Persian)* *"Dawn"*

You may see the name "Dawn," in this section, for notes. This has been considered an exotic and romantic name for centuries, and since she is now firmly fixed as the great love of Cyrano de Bergerac, she will probably stay that way, all Roxys to the contrary.

Stephanie *(Greek)* *"Crown"*

You may refer to the name "Stephen," among the boys' names, for an explanation, but it ought to be obvious by now, I think, who's going to claim the crowns in life. A variant form is Stesha.

ARIES
BOYS' NAMES

Boris *(Russian)* *"Warrior, fighter"*

The most martial and warlike signs of the Zodiac are Aries and Scorpio, especially Aries, who is ruled by Mars. (Who, to confuse people, is known as Ares in Greek.) Thanks to generations of humorous Russians in books and cartoons, Boris has a moderately comic ring today, but, due to the same fictional Russians, also continues to carry a slight air of pugnacious menace, which Aries will enjoy.

Buck *(English)* *"Male deer"*

A short, sharp, solidly masculine name that an Aries will find it easy to live with, Buck not only refers to the strong, vital animal, but also to a dollar, which is another of Aries's interests. And, just to seal the choice, buck is also a verb, something the Aries is known for doing. Mind you, there will be some predictable jokes about "buck naked." The pet form is Bucky.

Cyril *(Greek)* *"Lord"*

This is a name for the aristocratic egoists of the Zodiac, Aries, Scorpio, and Leo. It has suffered from years of use in the movies for ultra-refined Englishmen. It is sometimes used as a girl's name, too, which doesn't help. Generally, when a movie Cyril is not a wimp, he's the slimy villain. Sometimes he's both. But anyone lordly enough can carry it off, and if he should happen to drop a hint to the effect that it rhymes with "virile," so much the better.

Derek *(German)* *"Ruler of the people"*

This is another name for the aristocrats, Leo, Scorpio, and Aries, a trio about whom much will be said in this book. Derek is pretty popular these days—short, sharp names being considered masculine, impressive, and highly appropriate for heroes of paperback romances. The one drawback is spelling. Many people spell it "Derrick," like the building equipment. There is no accounting for taste.

Donald *(Celtic)* *"Mighty ruler"*

This is another of those names for Leo, Aries, and Scorpio, signs belonging to people who, if they aren't rulers, feel they deserve to be. You might think its popularity would have declined as a result of being identified with a duck, but there are a lot of people who like Donald Duck and identify with his brash manner and uncertain temper. (Do you suppose he's an Aries?) Pet forms are Don and Donny. Variant forms of the name include Donal and Dougal.

Eli *(Hebrew)* *"The highest"*

There's a bit of deity mixed in with this name, and Aries, Leo, and Scorpio would naturally claim it. An Aries would especially appreciate the fact that it's brief. Some prefer to spell it Ely.

Elmer *(German)* *"Famous"*

The sun signs who love the spotlight best are—how did you guess?—Aries, Leo, and Scorpio. Elmer Fudd sent this name into a nosedive. But Aries won't mind. Arians are unlikely to brood over things like this, and if they give it any thought at all, they will strive to become famous in spite of their name.

Everett *(German)* *"Strong as a wild boar"*

The signs of the Zodiac noted for physical strength are Aries, Taurus, Leo, Scorpio, and Sagittarius. Arians are also noted for strength of will, so it should fit them neatly. The pet form of this is Ev. Variant forms include Eberhard, Ewart, and Everard.

Garfield *(Anglo-Saxon)* *"Battlefield"*

Here is another for the warlike signs of Aries and Scorpio. It had a moderate popularity when James A. Garfield became president, and even more after he was assassinated. Now there's this cat involved, and it will probably spring up all over the place. A lot of people have intense admiration for a cat who does what he likes. The only fault I find hard to forgive is that he once came out with a name book.

ARIES

Guy *(German)* *"Warrior"*

This is another name for warlike Aries and Scorpio. Some name experts, or onomasts, prefer to think of it as meaning "sensible" or "guide," either of which should also fit Aries. A child named Guy will, of course, have to put up with people yelling, "Hi, Guy!" a remark which strikes them as high wit. You might prefer an alternate form of the name, like Guido and Guyon.

Harold *(Anglo-Saxon)* *"Ruler of the army"*

This is another warlike name, but Aries has some qualities of the officer that Scorpio lacks. Yes, you're going to tell me that people do not think "warrior" when they hear "Harold." Well, the pet forms are Harry and Hal, which ought to be macho enough for anyone. Harald is a variant spelling that may look a little more impressive.

Harvey *(French)* *"Bitter"* *(German)* *"Warrior"*

A lot of onomasts go even deeper, coming up with meanings like "Bitter warrior" or "Ardent and battleworthy" and even "One who will fight bitterly, to the death, for his homeland." At any rate, it seems to fit in with the Aries or Scorpio image. Other forms of the name are Harve, Hervé, and Hervey. Harvey is also the name of an invisible rabbit. There are worse things to be named after.

Herbert *(German)* *"Bright warrior"*

Aries and Scorpio are the martial signs, as hinted above, but Aries is also a fire sign, so the bright warrior was put here. Forms include Herb and Herbie. Now, I can hear you muttering, "These are warrior names? Harold? Herbert? Harvey?" Well, yes, they're warrior names. That's part of the problem. Parents who liked the warlike sound bestowed the names on unwarlike children, say, a Libra. The contrast was so funny to the easily amused that the name itself suffered by the comparison. Aries is strong enough, however, to overcome the humorous connotations.

John *(Hebrew)* *"God's gracious gift"*

No, I do not intend to insist that John is best suited to Aries alone. I am putting John here because Aries is the first chapter in the book and I want to get John off my chest. "God's gift" and similar meanings make up one of the most common groups of names. It is obviously your call whether your little bundle of joy is a gift from God or not. Don't sweat it; you'll change your mind a hundred times over the next twenty years. Enough names meaning "Gift of God" exist that I have sprinkled some into each chapter of the book; they can go anywhere.

Just a few of the forms of John are Johnny, Jean, Sean, Ian, Jonathon, Jon, Johannes, Giovanni, Ivan, Yves, Jan, Hans, Jock, Zane, Owen, Ewen, Janos, Juan, and Shane. There are plenty more. For some of the feminine forms, see Jane (Virgo girls).

Keith *(Celtic) "Forest, battlefield"*

The name experts get a little mixed up on this, but they all seem to agree there are trees and soldiers involved in it somewhere. Until they make up their minds, it should go to warlike Aries and Scorpio or to the outdoorsy Sagittarius.

Kent *(Celtic) "White, bright"*

As mentioned before, Aries is one of the fire signs. Aries is the type to burn bright with ambition. Kenton is a variant form with a minor following.

Lewis *(German) "Famous in battle"*

Some experts prefer to translate it "famous holiness." Aries is the warrior type, and likes the idea of being famous, too. The name seems to have been very popular, and variant forms abound. Some of them are Luis, Aloysius, Ludovico, Ludwig, Luigi, Lothar, Lou, and Louis. The "looey" pronunciation is becoming rather low-class, the more refined speakers preferring "lewis." I learned this the last time I was in St. Lewis, Missouri.

Mark *(Latin) "Warlike"*

This seems to be another choice for Aries and Scorpio, the warlike signs. The name Mark and the name for March are so closely related that this was the obvious place for it. A fraction of the population prefers to make it Marcus, with the short form Marc.

Maynard *(German) "Strong and brave"*

The experts aren't as unanimous on this meaning as I'd like, though they all agree on the "strong" part of it. The strong signs of the Zodiac are Aries, Scorpio, Leo, Taurus, and Sagittarius.

Michael *(Hebrew) "Who is like God"*

That is not a question; the name implies Godlike qualities. This is a tall order, but a Leo, Aries, or Scorpio will rise to the challenge. Aries will also fit in with the spunky qualities given the form Mickey by Mickey Rooney and Mickey Mouse. Other variant forms are Mick, Mike, Mikey, Michel, Miguel, Mikhail, Mischa, Mihiel, Mitchell, and Mitch. Mitchell is a name that belongs in a boardroom.

Percival *(French) "Pierce the valley"*

The implication is that a war leader can lead his men down into the valley and just generally wreak havoc. This makes it another warrior name and throws it to Aries and Scorpio. Percy has suffered a lot from the humorists, and it is only fair to mention that an Aries named this will get a goodly share of black eyes (and give them).

Ramsay *(German) "Ram's island"*

There can't really be any argument on this one, can there? This is another name that looks good at the top of a letterhead. Some people prefer the spelling Ramsey. The short form, Ram, got a push from Judith Krantz not too long ago.

Reed *(Anglo-Saxon) "Red-haired"*

Redheads are considered hot, spicy, impulsive people, just the sort of thing for Aries, Leo, Sagittarius, and Gemini. They are also considered unlucky. Some are and some aren't. The form Reid is used by a certain sort of people.

Richard *(German) "Powerful ruler"*

This is another lordly name for Aries, Leo, or Scorpio. It is a very popular name, probably because of Richard I, "the Lionhearted," King of England. Short forms are Rich, Rick, Ricky, and Dick. Ricardo is another form.

Roderick *(German) "Famous ruler"*

Another lordly name, this one also includes fame, making it just right for Leo or Aries. It can be shortened to Rod, Roddy, or Rick.

Ronald *(Anglo-Saxon) "Powerful"*

The onomasts come up with a lot of different ways to translate this, but all include implications of a mighty force. Aries and Scorpio are a couple of the most irrepressible characters in the Zodiac. The name got a powerful boost when Ronald Reagan was president. Another form of the same name is Reginald. Variant forms of these two include Ron, Ronnie, Reg, Reggie, Reynold, and Rinaldo.

Roy *(Gaelic) "Red" (French) "King"*

The onomasts are about evenly divided on which meaning of the name should be considered the one and only original one. Red is the chief color attributed to Aries, and Aries wouldn't mind being a king, either, so both meanings can be applied here.

Stephen *(Greek) "Garland, crown"*

This is another name for those kings of the Zodiac, Aries, Leo, and Scorpio. It abbreviates to Steve or Stevie. Alternate forms include Étienne, Stefano, and Steven. Many people prefer the Steven spelling because there are knotheads all over who insist on pronouncing the "ph" spelling as "Steffen" or "Stefan."

Vernon *(Latin) "Flourishing"*

This is a spring name and Aries, if you haven't lost sight of it amid the clashing spears of the preceding names, is a spring sign. Other forms of the name include Vern and LaVern. A feminine form is Verna.

ARIES

Vincent *(Latin) "Conquering"*

This comes from the same general word root as "invincible," and is another war sign for Aries and Scorpio. It can be used as Vince and Vicente.

Wilmer *(German) "Famous, resolute"*

Leo and Aries love fame, and can also be exceedingly resolute (stubborn). The name has not been in good repute since it was used for the vicious but ineffectual gunman in *The Maltese Falcon*, but this is a problem that won't come into play on the playground. More troubling might be the way it sounds like Wilma (not a variant). Maybe you can get around that somehow.

TAURUS
the Bull
April 22 to May 21

The word for the bull is bovine. Taurus is calm, patient, stubborn, phlegmatic, solid, stolid, stable, and frankly, just a bit boring. Taureans are the responsible, traditional, conservative plodders who never take risks, depending on endurance rather than originality or swift footwork. They are hopelessly inflexible. If they were record albums, they'd be in the Easy Listening bin. They incline to a thick, heavy build, and had better watch that second éclair at dessert time.

Slow, steady, good-humored, often shy, they are, however, relentless. Once they decide what they want, they can be reasoned with, but not pushed around. They will make money. Once made, the money stays with them. They are possessive, with things and with people. One of their chief attributes is what the experts call "prudent self-interest." They take care of things, and themselves.

I am told by the experts that Taurus, the bull, is a feminine sign of the Zodiac. I do not want this explained to me. I just thought I'd mention it.

Semi-famous Taurus types include L. Frank Baum, Peter S. Beagle, Leslie Charteris, John Collier, Thomas B. Costain, Walter de la Mare, Gardner Fox, Mell Lazarus, Anita Loos, Ngaio Marsh, Talbot Mundy, Sigrid Undset, and Kurt Wiese.

TAURUS
GIRLS' NAMES

Ada *(German)* *"Prosperous, happy"*

The sun signs most often associated with prosperity are Leo, Taurus, and Capricorn. Leo and Taurus are more inclined toward happiness, however, than the saturnine Capricorn. Adelaide is the original form of this name, and the number of variants is ridiculous. Some of them are Adela, Adeline, Addie, Addula, Addala, Adliz, Adelais, Adella, Della, Del, Lina, Adelicia, Adelice, Adelinda, Aline, Ellie, and Heidi. Some people also include Alice.

Agatha *(Greek)* *"Good"*

Naturally, any child can be good. Some just have to work harder at it than others. The ones who seem most inclined to behave themselves are Taurus, Cancer, Leo, Libra, Capricorn, and Pisces.

Alice *(Greek)* *"Truth"*

But heavy sentiment also leans toward making it a form of Ada (see above). All Alices have to cope with being compared to Alice in Wonderland. That Alice seems to have been a very down-to-earth chlid, and I'll wager she was a Taurus. Variant forms of Alice include Alicia, Alisha, Alyce, Alisson, Allison, Ali, Alix, and, they tell me, Elyssica.

Bernadette *(German)* *"Bear, courage"*

There are some animals that go deep into our folk history; the bear is one of these. Bears are big, ponderous, moderately intelligent, strong, and impressive. What really inspires the mystic awe of them among primitives is the way they sometimes walk on their hind legs, a sign of superiority humans like to reserve for themselves. They became a symbol of strength and courage, which describes Taurus well. The masculine form of this is Bernard; feminine forms include Bernardine and Bernetta.

TAURUS

Blossom *(English)* *"Blossom"*

This is obviously a spring name. For reasons not fully known to me, it is also a name traditionally bestowed upon cows, so I have included it in Taurus.

Bridget *(Celtic)* *"Strong, resolute"*

The name experts have been fighting about this one, but they agree that "strong" comes into it. The physically strong signs of the Zodiac are Aries, Taurus, Leo, Scorpio, and Sagittarius. In the days of widespread Irish-bashing, a century ago, Bridget lost some of its impact, being taken as a generic noun for any a) domestic servant, or b) Irishwoman. It has been coming back, mainly in its more exotic forms, including Brigid, Brigitte, Birgitta, and Bedelia. Pet forms include Biddy, Bridey, Britt, and Brie.

Chelsea *(Anglo-Saxon)* *"Port"*

A port is a safe refuge for persons on the seas. People born under Cancer and Taurus are the most likely to be regarded as refuges by other people. No one has explained to me why Chelsea should be used as a first name, though it is pretty. I suspect a relationship to Chessie, the kitten who does advertising, with her eyes shut, for the Chesapeake and Ohio Railroad.

Chloe *(Greek)* *"Newly blooming"*

This is another spring name, for Aries and Taurus. There's a love song about Chloe that used to be fairly popular, but is now heard almost solely in the Spike Jones version.

Constance *(Latin)* *"Constancy"*

We don't use the word constancy any more, but it refers to one who is loyal, faithful, and trustworthy; someone like a Taurus. Connie is the preferred pet form. Constanza and Constantia are variant forms. I have not seen a Constantina, but there must be one; Constantine is the masculine form. Constantinople (Constant City) should not be used as a first name, so don't even think about it.

TAURUS

Dorothy *(Latin) "Gift of God"*

For notes on "Gift of God" names, see John, under Aries boys, and Jane, under Virgo girls. The Dorothy who went to Oz, like Alice in Wonderland, seems to have been a marvelously calm creature, given all she had to go through. There are lots of variant forms: Dora, Dot, Dottie, Dodie, Doretta, Dorothea, Dorotea, Dasha, and Dodo.

Esmerelda *(Greek) "Emerald"*

For some reason, Esmerelda is a more popular form than Emerald, as a name. The emerald is believed to have many useful properties: it is thought to be soothing to the nerves, and a cure for sore eyes. This would seem to lend it more to Libra. But the emerald is also the traditional birthstone for May, so it goes here. (By the way, I hear that the list of traditional birthstones was made up at a jeweler's convention in Kansas City in 1912. I don't know; that's just the story that's been going around.)

There is a variant form that is mentioned in the name dictionaries for reasons best known to the onomasts. You may name your son or your daughter Smoragdus if you like, but don't expect me to be a party to it.

Georgia *(Greek) "Farmer"*

The feminine form of George, of course, and just the sort of thing for an earth sign, which is what Taurus is. Feminine forms of masculine names always give rise to a host of variants, and here you can have Jorja, Georgette, Georgina, and Georgiana, to name only a few. Some Georgias are named after the state, of course. Try to confine this sort of thing to Georgia or Virginia.

Hermione *(Greek) "Of the earth"*

The earth signs are Taurus, Virgo, and Capricorn. There is a lot of arguing about which names are variants of Hermione and which ones aren't. We can leave that to the experts. Some of the possibilities they mention are Erma, Irmina, Armonia, Harmonia, and Ermine.

Hortense *(Latin) "Gardener"*

This is another good name for the earth signs, Taurus being the one most likely to stay home and tend to her garden. I would be derelict in my duty if I did not point out that any name beginning with "hor" is going to provoke unseemly humor.

Laverne *(French) "Spring"*

This is another name that ought to go to Aries, Taurus, or Gemini in honor of the season. It is applicable to boys or girls, and is prone to arguments about where to put a capital letter (Laverne or LaVerne) and whether or not to put an "e" on the end. You may do as you like.

Megan *(Anglo-Saxon) "Strong"*

The physically strong signs of the Zodiac are Aries, Taurus, Leo, Scorpio, and Sagittarius. Megan has an Irish tinge to it, though, and seems to belong to spring, when things are green and earthy. Pronunciation seems to be a matter of personal preferance. Meg-An is in the ascendancy, but Mee-Gan and May-Gan have their following. Some ultra-Celts insist on Mee-Yan. Some people spell it Meagan, and heaven knows how they pronounce that.

Melinda *(Spanish, Greek, Latin, or something)*
"Soft, kind, and gentle"

The onomasts are always at their worst when they come up against a name with "lind" in it. They generally agree that Melinda has gentle overtones, though, so it should probably go to one of the gentler signs: Taurus, Cancer, Libra, or Pisces. Pet names for it include Mindy and Mandy.

Miranda *(Spanish) "Admirable"*

You might be inclined to give this, with the other complimentary names, to Leo, Aries, and Scorpio, who are prone to worshipful titles. But this doesn't imply worship, just admiration, which is a quieter, less fanatical sort of feeling. Taurus seems to bring that out in people; it's a good, solid sign, but no one gets very excited about it.

Norma *(Latin) "The pattern, normal"*

They insist this is not a feminine form of Norman, but a separate name. Taurus, Capricorn, Cancer, and Virgo, are most inclined toward traditional, regular lives. Noreen is a variant form.

TAURUS

Patience *(English)* *"Patience"*

Obviously. Taurus is chock full of this. You can use Pat as a short form.

Phyllis *(Greek)* *"Green leaf"*

This is another spring name, for Aries, Taurus, and Gemini. You might reach back to Pisces and give her a few spring names, too. There's nothing like an early spring.

Pia *(Italian/Spanish)* *"Pious"*

Your perception of this sort of name depends on what you think of the devout. Scorpio and Taurus seem to be the signs implying the deepest religious convictions, with Cancer and Capricorn close behind.

Poppy *(English)* *"Poppy"*

The poppy is a very symbolic flower. It represents sleep, an anesthetic, and a memorial to veterans of foreign wars. These are all things Taurus would approve of, and, in fact, the poppy is also one flower used to symbolize Taurus. There is a touch of illicitness lent by the opium poppy, but a Taurus might not notice.

Ramona *(German)* *"Mighty protector"*

Cancer and Taurus have protection on the brain; they can't seem to help themselves. Mona is sometimes used as a pet form. Raymond is the masculine version.

Rhea *(Latin)* *"Poppy"*

You may refer to the name Poppy, above, but, actually, the name experts have never agreed on this one. The party that says "Poppy" is just slightly ahead of the group that insists on "Mother," inasmuch as the original Rhea was the mother of the classical gods. She is considered to be a personification of Earth. Taurus is an earth sign, of course, so that ought to fit. Other experts prefer to translate the name as "free-flowing" or "a stream flowing from the earth." These things can go on for years. Don't wait up.

TAURUS

Rochelle *(French)* *"Little rock"*

This seems to be another tribute to the stubbornness of Taurus, unless, of course, you come from Arkansas, in which case it's free to all sun signs. Some people class it as a variant form of Rachel.

Rosalind *(Spanish)* *"Beautiful rose"*

As with all names including "lind," this one gets a certain amount of debate. But most of the onomasts go along with the beautiful rose. The rose, along with the poppy and the violet, are traditionally considered Taurus's flowers.

Sophronia *(Greek)* *"Of sound mind"*

You don't see the Sophronias around that you used to. Around 1830 there was a slew of them, particularly on the frontier. The name lingered for a couple of generations and then sort of slipped into obscurity. Of course, it just takes one rock singer named Sophronia to bring it roaring back. Taurus is the most level-headed of signs, though I'd have to admit it wins the title largely by default. Pet names for Sophronia include Sophy and Phronsie. Some people prefer to spell it Sophronisba. They're just asking for trouble.

Tansy *(Latin)* *"Tenacious"*

This is another nice word people use instead of "stubborn." People are tenacious when they're on your side, and stubborn when they're on the other side, see? All the signs can be stubborn, but Taurus is a natural.

Ursula *(Latin)* *"Bear"*

You may refer to the remarks on bears under Bernadette, in this section. Pet forms of this include Ursa, Ursel, Ursilla, Ursina, and Orsola. I wouldn't advise you to use any of them.

Zenobia *(Arabic)* *"Father's ornament"*

Several onomasts try to derive this from Greek, getting Zeus into it, mainly because of the "Z," I suspect. Either way, it's more of a tribute to the father, really, than the daughter. Pisces, Capricorn, Cancer, and Taurus are most likely to be proud of being Daddy's girl. Zena and Zenia are short forms of the same thing.

TAURUS
BOYS' NAMES

Arthur *(Celtic) "Bear"*

Oh, the experts have been at this name for centuries, and I want no part of it. The majority seem to lean toward "bear" these days, and since I am stuck on bears (see remarks under Bernadette, in Taurus girls), I'll go along with them. Pet names for Arthur include Art and Artie, while variants are Arturo, Arth, and Artus. The mystically-minded may wish to note that Artus is very nearly an anagram of Taurus. And they may not.

Bartholomew *(Aramaic) "Son of the plowman"*

Another farming sign for earthy Taurus. In these hectic days, we tend to frown on any name four syllables long, but Bart is very popular, very macho. Other forms include Barth, Bartolomé, Bartol, Bartlet, Bartleby, and Bartek.

Bernard *(German) "Courage of a bear"*

Robert Van Gulik wrote that bears, though brave and intelligent, were not original thinkers. This is another bear name for Taurus (please refer to Bernadette in Taurus girls). Related names are Barnard and Bernhard.

Brock *(Anglo-Saxon) "Badger"*

Not to get away from bears, but there are other animals that can represent Taurus. The badger is best known for being impossible to dislodge once he takes up a position. He digs into the earth and holds his ground, woe be to all attackers. Sounds like Taurus to me. This name is experiencing a minor surge just now because it is the sort of short, sharp name beloved of those who write soaps and paperback romances.

TAURUS

Byram *(Anglo-Saxon)* *"Cattle yard"*

This sounds like a good place for Taurus to me. Of course, with all the bulls and bears in this chapter, you might think he belonged in the market. (I had some idea of making a joke about stockyards and stock markets, but I have decided to leave it alone.)

Byron *(French)* *"Cottage"*

Taurus and Cancer are the most amenable to the modest, homely atmosphere of a cottage. If you're thinking of the poet, however, you would do better to take this name over to Scorpio. Byron was one of the early promoters of the Scorpio character in story and song. They called them Byronic heroes.

Edmund *(Anglo-Saxon)* *"Prosperous protector"*

Cancer and Taurus are the guardians among the characters of the Zodiac, and Taurus is one of the more prosperous signs. The pet name for this is Ed or Eddie, of course. A few onomasts consider the Irish name Eamon to be a variant, though others consider it a separate name meaning "fortunate warrior."

Farley *(Anglo-Saxon)* *"Bull pasture"*

Not all the names in this book were this easy. By the way, one of the experts I ran into insisted this means "Ram pasture," which just goes to show you.

Garth *(Norse)* *"Groundskeeper"*

Another guardian name, for Cancer or Taurus. Taurus, being the earth sign, might be a better choice. A variant form is Garrett.

George *(Greek)* *"Farmer"*

This is another name for the earth signs. (Virgo and Capricorn are the other two.) There have been lots of famous Georges; it seems to be that sort of name. Variant forms include Giorgio, Georges, Jorge, Georg, Joris, Iorgos, Jevry, Yuri, Igor, Geordie, Jorgan, and Yurik.

TAURUS

Godfrey *(German)* *"God's peace"*

Libra, Cancer, and Taurus are the most peace-loving of signs. Variant forms include Giotto and Gottfried, but the most popular is Geoffrey.

Goodman *(Anglo-Saxon)* *"Good man"*

Taurus is always a good bet for a name this straightforward. Besides, this is just the compliment Taurus is likely to get through life. "Yup, we've got a good man there," the boss will say, and then forget all about him. See Miranda, under Taurus girls.

Hector *(Greek)* *"Steadfast defender"*

Cancer and Taurus are the defenders in the Zodiac. Hector was one of the great heroes of the Trojan war, but just try to find anybody who gives a bad penny for that. He was famous a generation or two ago in the phrase "when Hector's dog was a pup," referring to some period a long long time in the past. It was an unwieldy phrase, though, and was eventually shortened to "when Hector was a pup," which didn't really matter unless someone asked who Hector was, and what kind of dog. Hector was not the dog, but the dog owner. Again, you'd have to walk pretty far to find anybody in this day and age who cares, but you'll need to know these things if you intend to name the lad Hector. Variant forms are Ector, Etor, and Ettore.

Howard *(German)* *"Guardian"*

If you look close and squint a little bit, you can almost see how the word "guard" became the name "Howard." Another name for the Taurus and Cancer types, it also comes in the pet form Howie.

Jasper *(Persian)* *"Jasper"*

Jasper is a precious stone; the name may come from a Persian phrase meaning "treasure keeper." The stone itself is believed to be a fertility charm, and a sure bet to bring rain. All of this leans toward Taurus, a spring sign, an earth sign, and an expert treasure keeper. Casper and Gaspar are considered variants.

TAURUS

Kirby *(German) "Church village"*

This brings up more of those humble, homely images that Cancer and Taurus revel in.

Knute *(Norse) "Knot"*

This is another tribute to the stubbornness of Taurus, who will be considered a stick-in-the-mud, a bottleneck. Taurus won't mind, because he knows bottles need necks. Variant forms are Canute and Cnut.

Leland *(Anglo-Saxon) "Meadowland"*

This is another farm sign for Taurus. If you consider meadows peaceful, you may apply the name to Pisces, Cancer, or Libra as well. My experience is that some are and some aren't. Lee and Leigh are variants.

Miles *(Latin) "Soldier"*

You may have expected something like this to go under the warlike signs, Aries and Scorpio. But this does not seem to be translated "warrior," just "soldier." It's a matter of image. Warriors dash into battle with raised swords or spears. Soldiers drill a lot on dusty parade grounds and slog along muddy roads with heavy packs. They are solid, stolid people, grumbling a little, who follow orders. They sound like Tauruses to me. Milo is a popular variant.

Morris *(Latin) "Dark-skinned"*

Scorpio and Taurus are inclined to be dark, though Sagittarius is most likely to be out getting a tan. Maurice, Mauritz, and Moritz are variants.

Orson *(Latin) "Bear"*

I have taken no poll, but only snakes seem to have gotten into as many names as bears. The bear seems to partake of so many Taurus qualities that I have given all the bear names to Taurus. See Bernadette, among Taurus girls, if you skipped it the first time.

Orville *(French) "Golden city"*

Variant meanings make it clear that this golden city (or golden estate) belongs to the bearer of the name. Capricorn, Leo, and Taurus are the most likely to make that kind of income. Orvie is the variant form, but be sparing with it.

Peter *(Greek) "Rock"*

All the sun signs include a little stubbornness, but Taurus has the most rocklike resolution. Peter is widespread, and comes in many varieties, including Pierre, Pierrot, Pietro, Piet, Pietr, Petrance, Piotr, Peder, Pedro, Pierce, Parnell, Pete, and Petey. Oddly, there seems to be no common female form, though some make a go of it with Petra.

Quincy *(Latin/French) "Fifth"*

See also Quentin, under Leo boys. You may apply this to the fifth month, May, and give it to Taurus or Gemini, or to the fifth sign of the Zodiac, Leo. When it first came out, it was generally used for the fifth child, or fifth son. Most of the names indicating birth order have faded now, though you can still occasionally meet a Prima (first), a Septimus (seventh), or an Octavius (eighth). Tertius (third) still has some following.

Randolph *(Anglo-Saxon) "Wolf shield"*

This implies a brave protector. I will have more to say about wolves later on; I'm concentrating on bears in this chapter. Randall and Randy are common variants. People named Randy will have to cope with the slang adjective meaning "sexually active and how." The experts aren't sure why Randy is so honored, though some feel it derives from a Hindu word meaning a lecher.

Sherman *(Anglo-Saxon) "Shearer"*

This is another farm name that suits the characteristics of Taurus just fine, I think. See, a shearer has to grab a sheep that doesn't especially want to be grabbed, and hold it while shearing off its wool without nicking the skin.

TAURUS

It takes a certain amount of control. No, I haven't tried it, but I have a feeling it's one of those things that's even harder than it looks. I wouldn't know how to begin grabbing a sheep. Shermie is the pet form, and any name ending in "man" can be abbreviated to Manny, as well.

Warren *(German) "Game warden"*

Taurus and Cancer, as mentioned before, are the wardens, the guardians, among the signs of the Zodiac. You can extend this name to cover the woodsy Sagittarians as well.

Wilfred *(German) "Resolute peace"*

Taurus, Cancer, Pisces, and Libra are peaceful signs, and Taurus is the one most likely to insist on it.

Willard *(German) "Resolutely brave"*

The brave ones in the Zodiac are Aries, Scorpio, Leo, Sagittarius, and Taurus, and, as mentioned, Taurus wins prizes for resolution. Willard Scott seems to have rescued this name from the doldrums it fell into after the horror movie *Willard* came out.

GEMINI
the Twins
May 22 to June 21

It's got to be a cushy job, writing horoscopes for Geminis. They change so much from day to day that if your predictions don't come true, you can always blame it on their mercurial nature.

Geminis love variety. They're the original "Oh, I know! Let's paint the piano pink!" people. They are quick, eager, alert, and friendly. They're always up to date, though some people think they're shallow because they just skim off the newest and most trendy information from whatever they read. They like people. They will talk in class. They will talk out of class. They are flirtatious when young, but will grow out of it if it takes them eighty years.

Deep down, Geminis want to be introspective, but they can never manage it. Just as they're figuring out what they're all about, they change again and have to start over. They will try anything to get to know the "inner them," from Haiku to Tarot to collecting beer cans to writing piano concertos. But they get bored so easily they never finish.

Geminis tend to be quick, slender, and dexterous. They love to help people, and since charm is their middle name, why not set them to volunteer work? They loathe insincerity, and are never insincere themselves. Mind you, this doesn't help much. "I wasn't lying," you'll hear. "It's just that I've changed my mind since then."

They will despise traditional names, too. If you meet a child named Shawondalin, he may or may not be a Gemini. But you can bet his parents are.

Semi-famous Geminis include John Kendrick Bangs, Nicolas Bentley, Max Brand, Edward Bulwer-Lytton, Lin Carter, Dashiell Hammett, Hergé, Tom K. Ryan, Dorothy L. Sayers, Cornelia Otis Skinner, and T. H. White.

GEMINI
GIRLS' NAMES

Amaryllis (Greek) "Fresh, sparkling"

This is the name of the flower, of course. I think every flower ever named has been used as a girl's name at some point, with the possible exception of Bachelor's Buttons or Jack-in-the-Pulpit. Gemini has a fresh, sparkling personality.

Ann (Hebrew) "Grace"

The more graceful signs of the Zodiac are Gemini, Aquarius, and Virgo. Ann is a nice, simple name, so naturally people have been trying to fancy it up for ages. Variant forms include Hannah (probably the original), Anna, Annette, Nanette, Nan, Nancy, Annelle, Nanine, Anais, Annke, Anne, Ana, Anya, Nina, Nita, Anka, Netta, Nanny, Annabelle, Nance, Nanon, Ninon, Annie, Anita, Annushka, and Anezka. There are plenty more.

Avis (Latin) "Birdlike"

When people say "birdlike" they never mean someone who soars like an eagle or circles like a vulture. They mean songbirds, and they mean smallish, carefree things that fly gracefully on the wind and sing their merry little hearts out come spring. I know a few things about songbirds that curl my liver, but why bust up a perfectly good fantasy? Anyway, it sounds like a Gemini to me. Ava is a popular variant.

Bambi (Italian) "Child"

Gemini is very childlike in its eternal curiosity and eagerness, and it also has the energy and sprightliness of a young deer. Bambi would suit a Libra, too. The onomasts, by and large, do not include Bambi in their name books, and I'm a bit inclined that way myself, from strictly niggling considerations. Bambi, in the book, was a boy.

Beulah (Hebrew) "Married"

June is the month for marriages, being named after the Roman goddess

40

of marriage. So this should fit a Gemini or a Cancer well. It does come laden with other meanings, though, as it is used both as a term for the nation of Israel and as a term for a maid, particularly a black maid. Both of these meanings are growing a bit esoteric as time goes on, though.

Bonnie *(French/Scottish) "Pretty, sweet, good"*

This ought to go to someone with plenty of charm, a Libra or Gemini. The Scots pronounce it so that it sounds like "bony," but don't let this throw you. Different forms of the same name are Bonny, Bonniebell, and Bonita.

Charmian *(Greek) "Joy"*

Several onomasts suggest that this name endures because it looks as though it means "charm." Charm or joy, it's still fitting for a Gemini. It is also spelled Charmiane, and some people insist Charmaine is the same name. In fact, some people spell it Charmaine, but pronounce it Charmiane. Some people spell it Charmiane but pronounce it Charmaine. The world needs these people, I suppose.

Cleopatra *(Greek) "Fame of her father"*

This is more of a tribute to Daddy again, but the fame of the name itself is what matters. Only an Aquarius or a Gemini could pull this off, though a Scorpio might get away with it now and then. Cleo is the common nickname form, and Pat will also do in a pinch.

Honor *(Latin) "Honor"*

Scorpio and Leo are among the most honorable of signs, but Gemini is very strict about that, too. There are lots of different forms for this one: Honorine, Honora, Honoria, Honour, Nora, Noreen, and Norina.

Jasmine *(Persian) "Jasmine"*

This is another flower name. Its color, yellow, inclines it toward Taurus or Virgo. But its main claim to fame is its use for generations in perfume, and it has taken on an exotic tinge more suited to Gemini or Aquarius. Variants include Gelsomina, Yasmine, Jessamyn, and Jessamine.

GEMINI

June *(Latin) "June"*

Not much trouble here. Gemini and Cancer should get this. April and June, by the way, are the only major names that come from months. Yes, I know you have several friends named May and Augusta, and probably some Julies, but these names come from other places and only got on the month afterward. June is a nice solid name, though, for month or girl, though some people created the form Junietta just to be fancy.

Lilac *(Persian) "Lilac"*

Lilacs are associated with shades of blue, and blue is one of Gemini's colors.

Margaret *(Greek) "Pearl"*

The pearl is the traditional birthstone for June, which makes this another one for Gemini and Cancer. Margaret is also related to the name Daisy, but why go into that?

Margaret is probably one of the top ten names of all time for variant spellings and nicknames. Some of these are Marguerite, Margarethe, Margot, Margaux, Marlene, Greta, Meg, Madge, Midge, Gretchen, Gretel, Gerda, Marjory, Margery, Peg, Peggy, Rita, Maisie, Marge, Margie, and Moggy. You can probably make up your own; everyone else does.

Mavis *(Celtic) "Thrush"*

Personally, I find it suspicious that Mavis and Avis should be so closely related and yet come from different languages. Just one of those things, I guess. As mentioned heretofore, Geminis are flighty.

Missy *(English) "Young girl"*

I should think it pretty obvious that this comes from the word "miss," meaning a girl, but people have used it as a nickname for Melissa and Millicent for so long that the name experts have become confused. It is a quick, cheerful name suited to Gemini and Sagittarius.

Pearl *(Latin) "Pearl"*

I see no reason to dwell on the fact that the word also refers to things that are pear-shaped. The pearl is June's birthstone, as mentioned, so this goes to Gemini and Cancer. Some people prefer to spell it Perle, and I guess that's all right with me. Pearlie has a nice ring.

Philomela *(Greek)* *"Nightingale"*

This has not been widespread since, say, the eighteenth century, but there's nothing wrong with it. The most famous nightingale was the one belonging to the emperor. It pined away in captivity, but was able to thrive once it was set free. This sounds like a Gemini, Aquarius, or Sagittarius type. On the flip side of the coin, the nightingale was also considered a symbol of beauty and fickleness. It may come to the same thing. Philomena is an acceptable variant.

Rhoda *(Greek)* *"Rose"*

The rose is the flower of Taurus, but it is also the birth flower for June, which extends it to Gemini and Cancer. Rhode and Rhody are variants, and, of course, you can also use Rose, Rosa, Rosie, and so on.

Rhonda *(Welsh)* *"Loud, powerful river"*

This is not at all a popular name among the onomasts, despite the Beach Boys' song. It refers to a rushing, overwhelming force, the sort of thing Gemini, Aries, or Scorpio would identify with.

Sandra *(Greek)* *"Defender of men"*

This is the more popular form of Alexandra, which was very big in Victorian and Edwardian times (partially because both Edward's wife and Victoria were named Alexandra). Gemini and Aquarius are the types to consider themselves protectors of mankind. Sandy is the obvious nickname.

Satin *(English)* *"Satin"*

This fabric seems to imply all things sensuous and sinful, so perhaps it ought to go to Scorpio. On the other hand, it is also considered luxurious, the sort of thing Libra would like. But from my acquaintance with the stuff, all I can say for it is that it is the slipperiest fabric I ever tried to hang onto, and that is Gemini through and through.

GEMINI

Scarlet *(English) "Scarlet"*

Now, some onomasts claim this means the color, and others say it comes from a kind of fabric known as scarlet. Let's face it, though: anyone named Scarlet was named for Scarlett O'Hara, with touches of the Scarlet Woman and Miss Scarlet, the young lady in Clue who did it in the parlor with the candlestick (and Colonel Mustard). It can really only be considered suitable for a Scorpio or a Gemini.

Tabitha *(Aramaic) "Gazelle"*

The gazelle is a swift, graceful animal generally seen bounding hither and thither in documentaries. That sounds like Gemini all over (and Gemini generally is, too). Favorite variants include Tabby, Taberia, and Tabatha. We really must make an effort to spell these things correctly, people.

Talia *(Greek) "Blooming"*

This is a spring name, and fits well enough in Gemini for that alone. But in its original spelling, Thalia, it was also the name of the muse of comedy, which isn't bad either. They tell me the pet form of this is Tally, but I find it a little difficult to swallow.

Tara *(Celtic) "Tower"*

What this name means depends on who you are. To some it will always be the home of Scarlett O'Hara. To others it is the traditional home of the Kings of Ireland. To some it's just a tower, and to others it's an exotic name for a girl. Gemini can cope with all of these, and will probably enjoy telling people about all the different meanings.

Twyla *(English) "Woven of double thread"*

Some onomasts dismiss this as a fanciful form of "twilight," and I can see their point. But the majority lean toward the double thread theory, which makes it just right for Gemini.

Vanessa *(Greek) "Butterfly"*

Butterflies flutter thither and hither, and you never know where they'll go or what they'll do next. Gemini, no? Pet names for it are Nessa and Vanna.

Zelda *(German)* *"Indomitable battle maiden"*

This is actually short for Griselda, which, in spite of the battle maiden business, was a name symbolizing patience, humility, submissiveness, and a whole lot of other things once considered womanly virtues. Such an about-face can only belong to Gemini.

Zephyr *(Greek)* *"Zephyr"*

Zephyr is now used to mean just any breeze, but once it was the name of the west wind, which, if you remember the song, is a wayward wind that yearns to go where the wild goose goes, or something. (You can find all the words in the songbook, *Real Men Don't Sing "Feelings."*) Anyway, it was a symbol of freedom, which is the keynote for Gemini, Aquarius, and Sagittarius. Girls with this name may have trouble around poets, who can't resist rhyming Zephyr with heifer. Perhaps this is why the variant form Zephyrine turned up.

GEMINI
BOYS' NAMES

Adrian *(Latin)* *"From the Adriatic"*

This is a part of the Mediterranean Sea, an area known for culture, commerce, and war. It's a busy place, where things are always happening, and just the sort of place Geminis would be likely to hang out. Hadrian is a common form of the same name. The feminine form is Adrienne.

Angel *(Greek)* *"Messenger"*

Geminis and Sagittarians are the best people to use as messengers; they're quick and they just love carrying news. Angelo is another male form of the name, less likely to draw out jokes about angels. Angela, of course, is the best known feminine form.

Archibald *(German)* *"Bold"*

Gemini, Aquarius, Aries, Scorpio, and Sagittarius are the bold ones in the

Zodiac, the ones who will take chances. Short forms of the name are Arch and Archie.

Aubrey *(German) "Ruler of elves"*

This is a sort of a mystical name, for the Aquarius and Pisces types, but it depends a bit on your view of elves. If you expect them to be little people who live in hollow trees and bake cookies, then this is more of a Gemini name. More mystical forms include Oberon and Alberich.

Blair *(Celtic) "From the plain"*

A plain is a flat expanse of land on which a person can run free. This suits Gemini, Aquarius, and Sagittarius, the Zodiac's free spirits. On the other hand, plains also tend to promote horsemen, and mounted warriors, so you might want to ease it toward Scorpio and Aries.

Brendan *(Gaelic) "Little raven"*

If you know the raven only from Edgar Allen Poe, you'd be inclined to put this name in with the gloomier sun signs, Capricorn or Scorpio. But long before Edgar, the raven had other jobs in folklore, some of them mystic and menacing, and some of them loud and mischievous. Crowlike black birds who make a lot of noise seem to have reputations for being smart alecs all over the world, so this name belongs to Gemini, Aquarius, and Sagittarius.

Brice *(Celtic) "Quick-witted, alert, ambitious"*

I couldn't have put it better myself. Capricorn can claim a piece of this, on the grounds of ambition, but it sounds like Gemini clean clear through. Variant forms are Bryce, and, believe it or else, Brick.

Clarence *(Latin) "Bright, famous"*

Some people insist that this is just another form of Clare. Leo and Aries are the folks who are after the spotlight and the cover of *People* magazine, but Gemini likes that, too. Geminis are always going to do something great that will make them famous, just as soon as they get around to it. That's the catch.

GEMINI

Clifton *(Anglo-Saxon)* *"Town near a cliff"*

Gemini and Aquarius would love living on the brink. Some experts say Clinton is a variant of Clifton, and some just say maybe. Cliff is the nickname form.

Clyde *(Welsh)* *"Heard from afar"*

This is a river name, but though most river names can be given to either boys or girls, I have failed to turn up any girls named Clyde so far. The noisy signs of the Zodiac are Gemini, Leo, Aries, and Sagittarius.

Duane *(Celtic)* *"Strong little dark one"*

For some reason, this makes me think of the little people, living underground but coming out by night to do this, that, and the other. An awful lot of the little people, who have amazing powers, and an even more amazing lack of any idea how to apply them, are Geminis, I think. It's the Capricorns among them you have to watch out for. A Capricorn leprechaun is nothing to sneeze at.

Variant forms of Duane boggle the mind. I'm going to list Dwayne, DuWayne, DeWayne, D'Wayne, Dwain, Dewain, Duwain, and then stop. I don't know about Duveen, but it looks like it to me.

Dudley *(Anglo-Saxon)* *"People's meadow"*

Gemini and Aquarius are the signs inclined to take up causes in the name of "the people." Dudley Do-Right of the Mounties has had something to do with the lack of popularity of this name, but let's not forget that it starts out with "dud."

Ernest *(German)* *"Earnest"*

This means to be eager, enthusiastic, serious about something. Aries, Gemini, Leo, Scorpio, Sagittarius, and Aquarius are the types to throw themselves into a cause. Geminis are even more earnest than most. It's just that tomorrow they'll be earnest about something else. Variant forms include Erno, Ernie, Ernesto, Ernst, and Ern. The feminine form is Ernestine. The experts have Erna as a separate name.

GEMINI

Gavin *(Welsh)* *"White hawk"*

This depends on your perception of hawks. If you see them as grand, graceful bird aristocrats, you can give the name to Leo. If you see hawks as fierce carnivores, Scorpio. If you think of them as birds that are known for speed and for having to wear a hood so they aren't distracted, Gemini is the place. Variant forms are Gawen, Gawaine, and Galvano.

Gideon *(Hebrew)* *"Feller of trees, destroyer"*

Nowadays, this is just another term for a real estate developer. Gemini and Aquarius are the types of people who would say, "Well—you can't let a bunch of old trees stand in the way of progress."

Hubert *(German)* *"Bright mind"*

Gemini and Aquarius are the bright-minded ones in the collection known as the Zodiac. Gemini may have some troubles with application, but he is bright. Hubie and Hugh are short forms, while Hobart and Hubbard are variants. Avoid this last or he'll be asked about his cupboard as long as he lives.

Hyman *(Hebrew)* *"Life"*

Babies are not, as a rule, named after death, at least not since the Puritans hung up their buckled hats. The lively signs of the Zodiac are Gemini, Aquarius, Sagittarius, Aries, Scorpio, and Leo. Gemini is livelier than most, though Aries and Sagittarius would give him a run for his money. Variant forms include Hymie, Hyam, Manny, and Chaim.

Jay *(German)* *"Lively bird"*

The blue jay takes the role mentioned above under Brendan, the lively, noisy, smart-alecky thief. People know the blue jay is a dubious character, but they can't help liking him because he's so colorful. This is obviously something for Gemini or Sagittarius.

Kermit *(Celtic)* *"Free man"*

Gemini, Aquarius, and Sagittarius are all great lovers of freedom. Kermit the Frog has eclipsed most other famous Kermits and is a perfect example. (Well, he hasn't married Miss Piggy yet, has he?)

GEMINI

Lloyd *(Celtic) "Grey"*

Grey is a traditional color for Virgo and for Gemini. Gemini leans more toward the bluish and silver greys. I had someone explain to me once what the difference was between gray and grey. Grey, she said, is the color of a goose's feather; gray is the color of a battleship. It made sense to me at the time.

Milton *(Anglo-Saxon) "Mill town"*

The towns with mills are the ones that grew up to be county seats. They were busy places, centers of business, a crossroads where people from all over would meet. That's where Gemini likes to be: in the thick of the action.

Otis *(Greek) "Keen hearing"*

Gemini and Aquarius are the ones who have their ears cocked to get the latest scoop. Always watch what you say around a Gemini; if a Gemini hears it, everybody hears it.

Roosevelt *(Dutch) "Rose field"*

The rose is the flower of Taurus, but forget that. Anybody named Roosevelt is probably being named after Theodore Roosevelt, the Republican, or Franklin D. Roosevelt, the Democrat, still referred to in some circles as "That Roosevelt." Both were extroverted, multi-talented gents who generally went out and got what they wanted. Aries or Leo would be a good bet, but if you want a child to be named after both a Republican and a Democrat, why not Gemini? Rosie is the usual nickname.

Ross *(Celtic) "Promontory"*

This is a fancy word for a high piece of ground that makes a good lookout point. Gemini and Aquarius are the ones always on the lookout, particularly Gemini. If you pay attention to what you're doing, you might miss something better as it goes by.

Thomas *(Hebrew) "Twin"*

No problem here, is there? Nickname forms are Tom and Tommy. Variants include Tomas, Tomaso, Tamlane, and Tam. Tom is also a generic name for male cats (as opposed to Tabby for females). Thomasine and Thomasina are used as feminine forms, but have not had a lot of support.

Wendell *(German)* *"Wanderer"*

This depends on what you think of wandering. If you think of it as something done by people who aren't too sure where they want to be, give it to Cancer and Pisces, the more fuzzy-minded folks. If you take the gloomy view, and think of homeless, persecuted souls, give it to Capricorn or Scorpio. But if you think of people who wander because they like to travel, people who are always off on another trip, then you want Gemini, Aquarius, and Sagittarius. Wendell sounds like a cheerful name to me, so I have put it here.

Winthrop *(Anglo-Saxon)* *"Friendly village"*

The affable signs in the Zodiac are Aries, Taurus, Gemini, Leo, Libra, Sagittarius, and Aquarius. The implication of a village and numbers of friendly people seems to suit Gemini best. Win and Wynn are nickname forms.

Xanthus *(Latin)* *"Blond"*

Obviously, any baby can be blond. But be careful, any baby's hair color can change as it grows up. And if I know Gemini, it'll probably be changed intentionally. But, realistically, only an Aquarius or a Gemini could cope with having an X for a first initial. Feminine forms include Xantha and Xanthippe.

Zebediah *(Hebrew)* *"Gift of the Lord"*

See John, under Aries boys, for notes on "Gift of God" names. Zebedee is another form of the same name; Zeb and Zebe are the pet forms.

CANCER
the Crab
June 22 to July 21

Cancer is second only to Taurus as the great plodder of the Zodiac. But where Taurus was stolid, Cancer is just timid. Natives of this sign are obsessively self-protective—horoscope writers say a lot of things about "crawling into one's shell," as though this were Cancer the Turtle. Cancers are insecure, jealous, hypersensitive, and inclined toward self-pity. They lack self-esteem and, in general, enthusiasm. They just know that if they get excited about something, someone will take it away.

It is not a good idea to take things away from Cancers. They are a) maniacally possessive, and b) fanatically sentimental. These are the people who never throw anything away. Their closets brim with "collector's items," and their shelves sag with scrapbooks. Everything they own has a memory attached to it and belongs in a special spot in the collection. You've heard of those people who believe inanimate objects have souls? I bet they're Cancers.

It was a fight to find the experts saying anything nice about Cancers. Well, they do love home, mother, and apple pie. They are very imaginative (sure, they can always imagine what *might* go wrong). Although they hate crowds, Cancers do shine in a small, intimate audience, showing a great sense of humor if they're in the mood. They hate arguments, but they can be stubborn. They love history, literature, and drama, and are fatally attracted to all the wrong people, especially Scorpios. They tend to have long arms and large chests.

Semi-famous Cancers include Fred Basset, E. Clerihew Bentley, John Ciardi, Irvin S. Cobb, Pierre Culliford, Antoine de St. Éxupery, Finley Peter Dunne, H. Rider Haggard, Lafcadio Hearn, Dorothy Gilman, Fergus Hume, Mervyn Peake, Matthew P. Shiel, and Basil Wolverton.

CANCER
GIRLS' NAMES

Agnes *(Greek)* *"Gentle, pure, meek, chaste, kind, etc."*

Pisces and Cancer are the meekest signs of the Zodiac. Agnes seems to have picked up a lot of forms over the years, including Agneta, Inessa, Inez, Ines, Ynes, Nessa, Neysa, Anais, Annis, Annice, Anise, Una, Agness, Agnetha, and, if you please, Senga. There oughta be a law.

Alma *(Arabic)* *"Learned"*

This also means something in Latin, but no one's quite sure what it is. They're inclined to make it out to be something like "Bountiful, generous, and nurturing to the spirit." Its most common use is in the term "alma mater" for a university, which brings us back to learned again, sort of. Virgo, Libra, Cancer, and Capricorn have the most respect for education, research, and tradition. There are other things you can get at college which appeal more to the other signs.

Amata *(Latin)* *"Beloved"*

Why not give this to an insecure sign, say Cancer or Virgo or Pisces, for reassurance? Every little bit can't hurt. Being a simple name, it has naturally reaped hundreds of possible variants. Some of these are Amy, Ami, Aimée, Amia, Amada, Esme, Esma, Mandy, and Amabel (not at all the same as Annabel). Amanda is considered to be a form of it by some onomasts, though others translate it as "Fit to be loved." Amadeus is related; Armedia has been seen. You can find more on your own time.

Bronwen *(Welsh)* *"White breast"*

The breast is supposed to be Cancer's physical bailiwick. I'm sure I could go into psychological and emotional details, and expand on the topic considerably, but I won't. So there. Bronwyn and Bronyn are alternate forms.

Coral *(English)* *"Coral"*

This is a sea creature, and as such ought to go to one of the water signs,

Cancer, Scorpio, and Pisces. Its use in jewelry is considered a sign of a highly civilized people, since primitives prefer shinier things. Cancer and Pisces wouldn't shine in a primitive society either. Some people insist on the form Coralie, and some use Coralyn. Let them.

Cynthia *(Greek) "The moon"*

The moon is Cancer's ruling planet, despite the fact that Artemis/Cynthia/Diana, the goddess of the moon, was not the sort of person to bother with Cancer or its type of people at all. Cindy, sometimes called Cyndi, is the usual pet form.

Dolores *(Spanish) "Sorrows"*

This is one of the titles of the Virgin Mary, many of which became first names. It obviously belongs to our gloomier signs, Cancer, Capricorn, and Scorpio. Variants include Delores, Dolorita, Delia, Lola, Dolly, and Doll. Dolly and Doll don't sound as sorrowful as they might, but everyone has to cheer up sometime.

Glenda *(Gaelic) "Valley"*

Valleys are often seen as sheltered, peaceful places to withdraw to. Cancer, Libra, and Pisces are the types who want to withdraw. Glenna, Glennie, and Glynis are variants; Glen is the masculine form.

Gwendolyn *(Celtic) "White brow"*

This is apparently meant for someone fair of face. It has a soft, lilting air about it that a Cancer or a Libra would appreciate. Gwen is the usual short form, though some people prefer Gwyn, or Gwenda, or Wendy.

Hildegarde *(German) "Stronghold in time of war"*

Cancer and Taurus are the kinds of people you look to for refuge or comfort in hard times. Hilda and Hildie are pet forms of the name.

Ima *(Hebrew) "Mother"*

This is not popular among onomasts, who feel obliged to drag out the old tale of Ima Hogg. They have me convinced now that Ima really lived, and that she never had a sister named Ura. But they never get around to telling me just what the Hoggs had in mind when they picked out the name. You might want to take a lesson from this, though, if your last name is Hogg, Fink, Pepper, or something like that. Yma is an exotic variant. If you had Cancerian twins you could name one Amy and one Yma. But I wish you wouldn't.

Iris *(Greek) "Rainbow; messenger of the gods"*

I know all about Iris and the sorts of messages she carried for the gods, but I am passing over her for the flower, which is assigned as one of Cancer's attributes. Cancers have nothing against rainbows, either, though they do worry about where they'll hide the pot of gold in case they find it.

Ivy *(English) "Ivy"*

Ivy, like Cancer, is best known for clinging to things.

Jennifer *(Celtic) "White wave"*

The onomasts are not unanimous on this, but they all agree it means white something. (Except for one bloke who said it meant "smooth and yielding.") "White wave" seems to be in the majority, so it should oprobably go to one of the water signs, Cancer, Scorpio, and Pisces. Jenny is the short form, a name often given to wrens and mules.

Jesse *(Hebrew) "God exists"*

The experts say this is not just a form of Jessica, but a separate name, given to boys or girls, and capable of being pronounced in one syllable, or two. It ought to go to one of those signs whose members are devout: Scorpio, Taurus, Capricorn, Cancer, or Leo.

Kate *(Greek) "Pure"*

This is a variant of Katherine, but it has a considerable following as a name on its own. It is solid and sensible, the sort of thing Cancer or Taurus would appreciate. Karen and Katie, also forms of Katherine, would do nicely for a Cancer, too. Katy is a bit brisker, and perhaps goes better with Gemini.

The problem with all these things that are advertised as "pure" is that you never find out the answer to the question "Pure what?" Forms of Katherine probably go best with signs that are pure—that is, with a single major quality: Taurus, Aries, Virgo, Cancer, Sagittarius, Scorpio, Capricorn, or Aquarius.

Kimberley *(German) "From the meadow of the palace"*

This sounds like somebody who works in the fields for the king, something submissive, like a Cancer, Libra, or Pisces. The short form, Kim, can be used for boys or girls; Kimberley is used almost exclusively for girls. Other forms are Kimba Lee and Kimber Leigh. I have seen Kamber Leigh, which has a certain ring to it, but which was probably a typographical error.

Lavinia *(Latin) "Mother of Rome"*

I assume this means someone named Lavinia was mother of Rome, rather than that the name actually means this. Still, anything to do with mothers ought to go to Cancer. Variants include Lavina, Vina, and Vinnie.

Leigh *(Anglo-Saxon) "Meadow"*

This is another peaceful sort of place for Taurus, Cancer, Libra, and Pisces. Some prefer the spelling Lee.

Mabel *(Latin) "Lovable"*

This is a form of Amabel, which is a form of Amata, though some onomasts try to derive it from the French "ma belle," meaning "my lovely." This ought to go to a Pisces or a Cancer, who need the reassurance. Mind you, they will have to live with that poem about elbows on the table.

Magnolia *(English) "Magnolia"*

This has a soft, peaceful sound to it, just the sort of thing for Cancer, Libra, and Pisces. It is considered an aphrodisiac, too, and that can't hurt. Maggie is sometimes used as a pet form, but is usually reserved for Margaret.

Minerva *(Greek) "Minerva"*

Minerva was one of the names of the goddess of wisdom generally known as Athena. She was also the goddess of defensive warfare, the sort of thing Cancer and Taurus understand. Minnie, Minna, and Nerva are variants.

Miriam *(Hebrew) "Bitter, rebellious"*

Now, if you want to go with the meaning, you can give this to Gemini, Aquarius, or Scorpio. But those are not the signs to cope with a name that, in its many forms, is so traditional, so common. Much better to give it to Cancer, Capricorn, or Taurus, who will appreciate it. The main variant is, of course, Mary. There are many other variations—more than are necessary—including Marie, Maria, Mimi, Mariah, May, Mame, Mamie, Mae, Mayme, Marya, Mirrim, Miri, Mari, Merriam, and so on.

Modesty *(English) "Modesty"*

The Puritans were heavily into naming their children for abstract concepts; it kept them from having to honor the old Catholic saints. A few of these were nice enough to survive the obsession, and Modesty is one of them. The more modest sun signs are Taurus, Cancer, Libra, and Pisces. Variants of the name include Modeste, Modestine, and Modesta. If you wanted to make a joke of it, you could apply it to Gemini, who likes to be up on the latest modes. No, huh?

Rose *(English) "Rose"*

This is a flower for Taurus, and for the signs of June: Gemini and Cancer. But roses have been around for so long, and have acquired so many different meanings, it could go anywhere. There's "sub rosa," under the rose, which means secret. The rose is a symbol of the pinnacle of success, as when one says of, say, a fine pickle, that it is "the rose of all pickles." As usual with a name so short and so widespread, it comes in at least 57 varieties, including Rosa, Rosetta, Rosette, Roselle, Rosine, Rosita, Rosanine, Roseanne, Rosemary, Rosalie, Rosalind, Rhoda, Zita, and so on.

Ruby *(Latin) "Ruby"*

The ruby is the birthstone for July, for Cancer or Leo. As a gemstone, it is supposed to insure the wearer's safety, which would be reassuring to Cancer.

Samantha *(Aramaic) "Listener"*

The onomasts insist this is a form of Simon, not Sam. Though Gemini probably has the best hearing (see Otis, in Gemini boys), the best listeners of the Zodiac are Taurus, Cancer, Libra, and Pisces.

Selena (Greek) "Moon"

See Cynthia, in this section. Cancers are also known as Moon Children, particularly those people who are squeamish about the C word. Variant forms are Selene, Seline, and Selina. (But not Celine or Celina.)

Shannon (Celtic) "Little, old, wise one"

This conjures up visions of the elder of the tribe, a wizened old shaman, giving advice to the people, the sort of thing Cancer or Capricorn would be good at. It is also a river name, and, like most river names, is applied to both boys and girls. It has become very popular of late, in response to no impetus that I have noted. Some onomasts claim Shannon is just another form of John.

Taffy (Welsh/Hebrew) "Beloved"

Cancer and Pisces, as mentioned above, need all the TLC they can get. If you prefer to think the name means a kind of candy, perhaps Libra is the best bet. In Wales, where this is just a form of David, it is applied to both boys and girls. Over here, believe it or not, some people prefer to make it Taffine. (Toffee drinkers?)

Zona (Greek) "Belt, girdle"

Cancer and Virgo don't mind being held in by something; some of them prefer it. Another meaning for the name is "shingles," but we don't have to talk about that.

CANCER
BOYS' NAMES

Abraham (Hebrew) "Father of a multitude"

Cancer, Leo, and Capricorn are the most parental of the signs of the Zodiac. Abraham is also the name of a patriarch, and Capricorn or Cancer are most likely to appreciate the tradition behind it. Variants include Abe, Abie, Abran, and Bram. Some include Abram as well, though it is really a separate name.

CANCER

Alvin *(German) "Beloved by all"*

I can't guarantee that giving your Cancer or Pisces one of these "beloved" names will actually make them any chirpier, but we have to do what we can. Al is the nickname form of this, and Elwyn is a variant. Alvina and Alvena are feminine forms.

Anthony *(Latin) "Inestimable, priceless, beyond praise"*

This belongs to the signs that appeal more to the grandstand audience, Leo or Aries. But give Cancer a break; they may find it inspirational. The feminine form is Antonia. Masculine forms are Antonio, Antoine, Antony, and, of course, Tony.

Blaise *(Greek) "Stammerer"*

But this name is more for Cancer as he is, one of the great hesitaters of the Zodiac. Most boys named Blaise are named for the sorcerer who was Merlin's tutor. (This is where the action heroine Modesty Blaise got her last name.) Some people claim Belasius is an acceptable variant.

Bradley *(Anglo-Saxon) "Broad meadow"*

This is a name implying a great green peaceful field, just the sort of place Taurus, Cancer, Pisces, and Libra would appreciate. Brad is the nickname form, but it does offer ammunition to others, sounding so much like "brat."

Burton *(Anglo-Saxon) "Fortress"*

After all that has been said, you might not think of Cancer as a tower of strength. But when it comes to defending something, particularly when it is something he owns, or feels responsible for, he acquires the power somewhere. This holds true for Taurus as well.

Cameron *(Celtic) "Bent nose"*

There used to be a saying, "His nose is out of joint," for people who had been offended, particularly people who were feeling angry and jealous. Scorpio and Cancer are the signs most likely to be found in this condition.

CANCER

Daniel *(Hebrew) "God is my judge"*

You have a choice here in your interpretation. If you figure this message means "God *alone* can judge *me*," then give the name to one of the supremely confident signs: Aries, Leo, Scorpio, or Capricorn. But if you take it to mean "God is keeping an eye on what I'm doing," it goes to a more timid group, Cancer and Pisces. The pet names are Dan, Dan'l, and Danny. Feminine forms are Danielle and Daniella.

David *(Hebrew) "Beloved"*

You can, of course, give these "beloved" names to other signs; that's only natural. But giving one to an insecure Pisces or Cancer now might save money on the psychiatrist's bill later. Then, too, when Cancer is feeling oppressed and powerless, he can always reflect on the original David and what became of Goliath. Other forms of the name are Dave, Davey, Taffy, and Dewey.

Douglas *(Celtic) "Dark water"*

This is obviously meant for one of the water signs. Give it to Scorpio if you think this means water that is deep, unfathomable. Cancer should get it if you think of gloomy, shadowy lakes. But if it means water that's a bit muddled and hard to see through, give it to Pisces. This is another river name, and has been given to both boys and girls. The pet forms are Doug or Duggie.

Edward *(German) "Prosperous, happy guardian"*

Taurus and Cancer are the guardians of the Zodiac, as mentioned before. Pet forms of the name are Ed, Ted, Ned, Eddie, Teddy, and Neddy. Edmund, Edgar, Eduardo, and Edvard are variant forms.

Ezekiel *(Hebrew) "God will strengthen"*

This is just the sort of message a Cancer or Pisces needs during speed trials for the rat race. The pet form is Zeke, which has a sort of hayseed flavor to it. It may come from a belief that Biblical names like this were most prevalent among the farm towns of the Bible Belt.

CANCER

Gregory *(Greek)* *"Watchful"*

This is either someone who is on guard, or someone who is very nervous. Either will do for Cancer. Diminutive forms are Greg, Gregor, and Gore.

Ira *(Hebrew)* *"Descendant" or "Watcher"*

Taurus and Cancer, the Zodiac's guards, are the best choices for "watcher"; Pisces, Capricorn, Cancer, or Libra if you prefer the "descendant" meaning. "Watcher" may apply to Pisces as well; some onomasts insist it refers to someone who has visions. The name is also sometimes given to girls.

Joshua *(Hebrew)* *"God saves"*

This is another encouraging message to Cancer and Pisces, and, like David, it carries the connotation of succeeding against long odds. Pet forms of it are Josh and Josharu. Jesus is a variant form.

Kevin *(Celtic)* *"Kind"*

Cancer, Pisces, Libra, and Taurus are the kinder signs of the Zodiac. Kev and Kevvy are the nickname forms. A variant form which the onomasts have not yet picked up on as a nickname form is the one ending in "er," as in "Kevver" for Kevin, or "Danner" for Daniel. It's considered more macho than, say, Kevvy, but not as brusque as Kev.

Leif *(Scandinavian)* *"Beloved, descendant"*

This is another "beloved" name for Cancer and Pisces, and can be extended to Libra and Capricorn, who are proud of their ancestors. You may flip a coin as to pronunciation. Some favor "leaf" and some favor "lafe." "Life" is not considered acceptable, so far as I know.

Leslie *(Celtic)* *"Grey fort"*

This is another refuge in time of trouble, a job for which Taurus and Cancer qualify. It is given to both boys and girls, and can be spelled Lesley. (Apparently no one has gotten around to Leslee or Leslea yet.) The nickname form is Les.

CANCER

Logan *(Celtic) "From the hollow"*

The hollow ought to be a nice, sheltered place for Cancer, Pisces, and Libra to escape to when they're feeling put-upon. A few onomasts claim this has something to do with logs. I think they're guessing.

Lyle *(Latin) "Island"*

Cancer, Capricorn, and Scorpio are the signs most likely to try to disprove the old line about no man being an island. Cancer is more likely to enjoy solitude for its own sake; Capricorn and Scorpio are solitary because no one else measures up to their standards. A variant form is Lisle.

Marshall *(French) "Steward, housekeeper"*

And, of course, the marshal, that hero of westerns and keeper of the peace. It sounds like another job for those natural guardians, Taurus and Cancer.

Nathaniel *(Hebrew) "God has given"*

See John, in Aries boys, for notes on "Gift of God" names. Nat, Nate, and Nathan are short forms of this.

Obadiah *(Hebrew) "Servant of the Lord"*

Taurus, Capricorn, Cancer, and Scorpio seem to be the signs with the deepest religous convictions, for various reasons. Obed is a variant. Obie can be used as a nickname.

Parker *(Anglo-Saxon) "Park keeper"*

Cancer and Taurus can handle the guardian duties, though Sagittarius could also be considered, being an outdoors type of sign. This is another name that people like to see on letterheads and on brass plaques in business suites.

Raymond *(German) "Mighty protector"*

Cancer and Taurus are, as has been hinted, the sort to trust with defensive duties, and Cancer will appreciate the bit about being mighty. Ray,

Raymie, Raimon, and Ramon are variants. Ramonda and Ramona are feminine forms.

Roland *(German) "From the famous land"*

This name obviously belongs to a patriotic type, one proud of his tradition and heritage. Taurus, Capricorn, and Cancer are the signs most prominent in these areas. Rollie is the nickname form.

Ward *(English) "Guardian"*

This is another one of those names implying someone who keeps a watchful eye, a Cancer or Taurus name. The name has been getting some support from old "Leave It to Beaver" fans who always admired the way Ward Cleaver had a handle on things.

Wilbur *(Anglo-Saxon) "Beloved stronghold"*

Cancer is the home-lover of the Zodiac, the one who regards his palace as a stronghold to be cherished. Will and Willie are nickname forms.

Zachary *(Hebrew) "God has remembered"*

This is another message for the morose or insecure—Cancer, Pisces, Scorpio, Capricorn, or Virgo. Variants include Zacharias, Zachariah, Zechariah, Zach, Zack, and Zacarias.

LEO
the Lion
July 22 to August 21

No need to spend a lot of time on this one. Just think of lions (king of the beasts) and you'll get the idea. Or, if your experience with lions is minimal, think "BMOC," or "Big Man on Campus."

Leos are those dynamic go-getters who have to be boss, have to be smack in the center of the spotlight. They work hard, and they are habitual volunteers, frequently to be found doing community service. But there's a catch. A Leo will do almost anything for you as long as you applaud afterward. Leos who do not get applause become melodramatic and sulky.

A lot of people don't like Leos, who can be bossy and never have an ounce of tact. But Leos get over this; they'll buy friends if they have to. A Leo has to have an audience around.

Leos are tall, exuberant, optimistic souls who move through life with confidence, knowing that nothing very bad can happen to them. After all, look who they *are.*

Semi-famous Leos include Anthony Boucher, Roark Bradford, Dik Browne, Lord Dunsany, Harold Foster, Paul Gallico, Montague Glass, Georgette Heyer, Edward Hopper, M. R. James, H. P. Lovecraft, Don Marquis, Ogden Nash, Edith Nesbit, and E. A. Wallis-Budge.

LEO
GIRLS' NAMES

Amber *(Arabic) "Amber"*

Amber is fossilized sap. It has been regarded with awe for centuries, and, for all I know, there are people at this very moment sitting around regarding amber with awe. If you believe, with the ancients, that amber has healing powers, you may wish to give this to Pisces or Aquarius. If, however, you immediately think of the heroine of the once-scandalous novel, *Forever Amber*, you may prefer it for a Scorpio or a Capricorn. But if it just means a color to you, well, amber is one of Leo's colors.

Ariadne *(Greek) "Daughter of the sun god"*

Leo is ruled by the sun, which puts this name here. Ariane is preferred by some people, possibly because it sounds like Ann.

Augusta *(Latin) "Venerable, exalted"*

This obviously belongs to Leo, not only because she loves to be venerated, but because three weeks of August belong to Leo, after all. Variants are Augustine, or Gussie. Male forms are August, Augustus, Augustine, and Gus.

Camille *(Latin) "Young ceremonial attendant"*

The onomasts seem to agree that this is a title generally given to young people, male or female, who were chosen from among young members of good families to act as attendant at important temple ceremonies. The trick is to say this in as few words as possible, because onomasts do not have much faith in the attention span or intelligence of people who read name books. So the definitions run from "born free" to "noble and right- eous handmaiden of unblemished character." Anyway, it sounds like the kind of job Leo would love; pomp and ceremony are her meat. Camille is used as a boy's name in some parts, and Camilla is used as a variant. The nickname forms are Cam and Millie.

LEO

Candace *(Greek) "Glittering, glowing white"*

This belongs to the more burning of the fire signs, Leo or Aries. Candy and Candice are other forms of the name. It is generally pronounced in two syllables these days (Cand-iss), but I am informed that the original pronunciation had three (Can-day-see).

Cheryl *(German) "Manly"*

Now, this is the sort of thing that happens when you start making up female forms for male names. This is a variety of Charles, which means "manly," and the onomasts break down completely when it comes to translating the feminine form. Does it mean Cheryl is manly, too, or does the meaning change when the spelling does, to make it mean womanly? I am taking the easy way out, here, and using it as a girl's name under one of the masculine signs of the Zodiac. (The masculine signs of the Zodiac, in case you don't have them memorized, are Aries, Gemini, Leo, Libra, Sagittarius, and Aquarius.) I have always thought Cheryl sounded feminine, myself. Some onomasts try to dodge the question entirely by saying Cheryl is really a form of Cherie, or Charity, or even Cherry.

Daisy *(Anglo-Saxon) "Eye of the day"*

The daisy is one of Leo's flowers, being identified with daylight and the sun. Flower names are not as popular as they once were; they're too simple, somehow. This is why you will find forms like Daysey or Daizee.

Erica *(German) "Powerful, regal"*

This is the feminine form of Eric and, like it, belongs with the masterful signs of the Zodiac: Aries, Leo, and Scorpio. It has a number of pet forms, including Ricki, Riki, Rikki, and Rica.

Faith *(English) "Faith"*

This is another survivor from the Puritan age of abstract names. Leo abounds in faith, to the point of blind faith. Some onomasts say Faye is a form of this.

LEO

Goldie *(German) "Golden hair"*

This is another color identified with Leo and the sun. Golda and Golden are variant forms.

Harriet *(German) "Mistress of the home"*

Leo, Aries, and Scorpio are the bosses among the signs of the Zodiac. The masculine form, obviously, is Henry. Variant forms for women include Harriette, Hatty, Hetty, Hattie, Henrietta, Yetta, and Enriqueta.

Imogene *(Latin) "Image"*

Leo is always concerned with her image. This can be pronounced with a long or a short i. Imogen is a variant.

Josephine *(Hebrew) "God will add"*

This is something for the optimistic signs of the Zodiac: Leo, Aries, or Sagittarius. Joseph is the masculine form. Other forms include Josefina, Josepha, Fifi, Fifine, Josie, Jo, and Josette.

Joyce *(Latin) "Joyous"*

Joyce is another optimistic name for Leo, Aries, or Sagittarius. It is often given to boys as well as girls. Joy is a popular variant; some people have invented Joyva and Joysia.

Kalinda *(Sanskrit) "Sun"*

Leo is the sign of the sun. This is not a common name in my neighborhood, but it will probably catch on, since it blends nicely with all the Melindas and Belindas.

Louise *(German) "Famous in battle"*

Aries and Scorpio are warlike, but Leo is no slacker, and, like Aries, is after the fame. There are scads of forms of Louise, as there are of Louis. They include Lois, Heloise, Eloise, Louisiana, Louisa, Luisa, Lovisa, Aloysia, Lola, Lu, Lov, Lulu, Ludovika, Ludwiga, Lotharia, and so on and on and on.

Marigold *(English)* *"Marigold"*

Marigold is Leo's flower, too. Don't ask me. There are people who know these things, that's all.

Martha *(Aramaic)* *"Lady"*

Lady of the house, is what it implies, and this belongs to the boss signs of the Zodiac: Aries, Leo, and Scorpio. Some onomasts try to make it out to be another form of Mary, but most of us aren't buying it. Variants include Marta, Marthe, Mat, Pat, and Patti.

Michelle *(Hebrew)* *"Who is like God"*

This is the sort of challenge Aries, Leo, and Scorpio would eat up. The masculine form is Michael, of course, which is why so many Michelles are called Mickey, or Micki, for short. Other forms include Micaela, Miha, Midge, and Shelley.

Mona *(Irish)* *"Noblewoman"*

This also goes to the aristocratic Aries, Leo, and Scorpio. If you incline toward the onomasts who derive this from the Greek word for "one," you may give the name to Scorpio, the most solitary of the signs. Monique and Monica are variants.

Nola *(Celtic)* *"Noble, famous"*

Aries and Leo are not only aristocrats, but also spotlight hoggers. The masculine form, less popular, is Nolan.

Oriole *(Latin)* *"Fair-haired"*

Specifically, golden-haired, which makes it Leo's sort of thing. The songbird is not a bad choice for Leo either. Oriel is a variant.

Patricia *(Latin)* *"Noble, well-born"*

As noted in Patrick, in this section, this name makes it pretty obvious that you are from the right family, and can list your forefathers for generations, if you want to. Leo, Aries, and Scorpio are inclined this way. For such a high-sounding name, Patricia comes with an amazing array of chirpy little nickname forms: Pat, Patti, Patty, Patsy, Tricia, Trisha, and Trish.

Phoebe *(Greek) "Shining, brilliant"*

This was one of the titles of Apollo, Greek god of the sun, and obviously belongs with Leo. I am not prepared to suggest, however, that Apollo himself was a Leo. Though it's possible; he was always grouchy when he met someone who didn't appreciate what a great and marvelous person he was.

Quinn *(Anglo-Saxon) "Queen"*

Several onomasts try to make this out to be the feminine form of Quincy, and it can probably be used that way. But the "queen" meaning seems so obvious that it should probably go to Leo, Aries, or Scorpio, the folks with regal bearing.

Regan *(Celtic) "Royal"*

Regal, if you prefer. This is a form of Rex, by way of Regina, and is an obvious name for Aries, Leo, or Scorpio. In literature, Regan was one of the nasty daughters of King Lear.

Summer *(English) "Summer"*

This obviously belongs to a Cancer, a Leo, or a Virgo. Summer, Spring, and Autumn have been getting support as first names over the past decade. Winter doesn't seem to inspire anyone that way.

Theodora *(Greek) "Gift from God"*

See John, under Aries boys, or Jane, under Virgo girls, for notes on this kind of name. Theo is a short form. As several onomasts point out, this name is really just Dorothea flipped around.

Theophania *(Greek) "Manifestation of God"*

The most common form of this name is Tiffany, which adds its own challenge to the bearer. Leo and Aries are the most likely to be able to face this kind of expectation. Tiphaine is an alternate version, Tiff or Tiffy being the nickname forms.

LEO
BOYS' NAMES

Abner *(Hebrew)* *"Father of light"*

The onomasts are pretty iffy on this. They can all see "father" and "light" in this, but what does that mean? "Father of light"? "Father is light"? "Light of the father"? Until they get this cleared up, it may be best to hand it to one of the fire signs—Aries, Leo, or Sagittarius.

Ace *(Latin)* *"Unity"*

That's all very well, but its chief uses are to refer to the number-one card in the deck or an expert in his field. This second use is said by some to be a tribute to Asa Brainard, the first great baseball hero. Aries, Virgo, Cancer, Capricorn, Scorpio, and Leo are the types who strive to be the best there is at what they do, and Leo and Aries would be best able to carry off the jauntiness of a quick little name like this.

Ali *(Arabic)* *"The greatest"*

Well, what else? This is obviously a name for Leo or Aries.

Ariel *(Hebrew)* *"Lion of God"*

This isn't difficult to figure out, I hope. The name is sometimes given to girls, too, but that's sort of Shakespeare's fault. He wrote "The Tempest," in which a character named Ariel has a perfectly swell time, kidding around with the humans. Shakespeare buffs have never decided whether Ariel ought to be played as a male or a female, though, and women take the part on stage as often as not. There is also a tendency to consider names ending in "iel" feminine, *if* the "iel" is pronounced in two syllables. (Mur-ee-ell, you see, as opposed to Dan-yull.) A variant, Arel, may solve this problem.

Basil *(Greek)* *"Kingly"*

This goes to the lordly signs, Aries, Leo, and Scorpio. This can be pronounced with a long or a short "A," although whichever way you say it, someone nearby is going to wince and tell you you're wrong. A variant is Vassily.

Boyd *(Celtic)* *"Yellow, blond"*

All yellows and golds and shades in between are supposed to be the colors of Leo.

Caesar *(Latin)* *"Much hair"*

Yes, well, actually, anyone named Caesar is named for the family of Roman emperors. That's something Leo would like. In addition, the best known Caesars, Julius and Augustus, gave their names to July and August, Leo's months.

Cassius *(Latin)* *"Vain"*

That's right; why be subtle about it? A lot of Leos are stung to the quick when accused of vanity. "I'm not vain," they'll tell you. "Being vain is when you really aren't as great as you think you are."

Cyrus *(Persian)* *"King, sun"*

This implies a sort of super-king, a king equated with the sun itself. Fortunately, Leo is ruled by the sun, so he can probably handle the comparison. Cy is a short form.

Earl *(Anglo-Saxon)* *"Noble"*

This is pretty plain and straightforward, I think. It belongs to Aries, Leo, and Scorpio, the aristocrats.

Edwin *(Anglo-Saxon)* *"Rich friend"*

Of the prosperous signs, Taurus, Leo, and Capricorn, Leo is the most inclined to make friends. He is least likely to wonder if his friends like him for his money because he is least likely to care.

Elroy *(Latin) "King"*

This is another aristocratic moniker for Leo, Aries, and Scorpio. By switching the first two letters, you get a variant form, Leroy, which can be spelled in a variety of ways, including LeRoi, Leroi, LeRoy, etc.

Erroll *(German) "Nobleman"*

This is pretty obviously just "Earl" in another version and, like it, goes to Leo, Scorpio, or Aries.

Hiram *(Hebrew) "Exalted, noble"*

Keeping in mind, of course, that in this context noble generally means a person of high station, and not necessarily one who is high-minded and virtuous, we give this to Leo, Scorpio, and Aries again. I'm not insinuating anything about Leo, Scorpio, or Aries; I'm just trying to keep these things straight. The short form is Hi.

Lawrence *(Latin) "Laurels"*

Aries, Leo, and Scorpio are the sorts to strive for the laurel wreath indicating a champion. There are lots of variants: Lorenzo, Lorenz, Lauren, Lorne, Lon, Lars, Larry, and Lauritz, among others. The feminine forms are Laurel and Lorna.

Leo *(Latin) "Lion"*

I suppose you were able to figure this one out for yourself. Leo is the only sign that really makes it as a first name. You could use Gemini for a girl, I suppose, and call her Gem. (There's always Gemini Cricket as an example.) And perhaps Capricorn, shortened to Cap, would give the right child a sort of an air. But don't let me catch you naming the kid Cancer; there's no excuse for that, no matter how you feel about it.

Leon is a variant form, as are Lev, and, according to some, Napoleon. Leona and Leonie are the feminine forms.

Lionel *(Latin) "Lionlike"*

One or two onomasts try to make this out to be "lion of God," like Ariel, because of the "el" on the end. But the majority put that aside and make it an adjective form of Leo.

Luther *(German) "Famous warrior"*

Leo likes the fame, and is not behindhand in war, though Aries and Scorpio are more warlike. This is itself a variant of Lewis; other versions are Lothar, Lothaire, and Lothario.

Maximilian *(Latin) "The greatest"*

"To the max," in other words. This is for Leos who want something a little more elaborate than "Ali."

Melvin *(Celtic) "Chief"*

This is another name for the leaders, Aries, Leo, and Scorpio. Melville is a variant. Melville Dewey, the famous librarian, went into spelling reform and introduced Melvil as the version of the future. He is known as Melvil Dewey to this day, but I haven't found anyone else who picked up on the spelling.

Owen *(Greek) "Well-born"*

This suggests the patricians of the Zodiac, the omnipresent trio of Aries, Scorpio, and Leo. Some onomasts feel that Owen is really just another form of John.

Patrick *(Latin) "Nobleman"*

If you've been paying attention, you'll notice that I keep using "patrician" as a synonym for "nobleman." This is where that sort of thing comes from. Leo, Aries, and Scorpio are the patricians. You might get away with calling a Leo Pat or Paddy, but do not attempt this with a Scorpio unless you are sure of your ground. Patrice and Padraic are variants. Patricia is the feminine form.

Quentin *(Latin) "Fifth"*

This can go to the fifth month (it's May; don't bother counting on your fingers) or Leo, the fifth sign of the Zodiac. See Quincy, under Taurus boys.

Ralph *(Anglo-Saxon)* *"Wolf-counsel"*

Leo, Virgo, and Capricorn are always going around giving advice, or counsel. Putting "wolf" on the front is supposed to suggest that the advice being given will be wise. The wolf is another one of those predators that haunted the imaginations of people who lived in their territory. Their power and cunning inspired awe and fear, but not much affection. Charlotte Yonge calls the wolf "the model of the marauder," and this is pretty much how it struck our ancestors. Nowadays, we have researched these things and have discovered that wolves are nice enough sorts, who mate for life and make affectionate parents. For myself, I suspect our ancestors knew this, too. But the knowledge that wolves lead exemplary home lives is very little consolation if you're missing sheep. At any rate, the impression the wolf made resulted in his appearance in numerous names. Ralph comes in a lot of varieties, including Raul, Raoul, Rollo, Rudolph, Radulph, Rolf, Rolfe, Rollin, Rollie, Randolph, and Raphael.

Reuben *(Hebrew)* *"Behold a son"*

This kind of fanfare would be relished by Leo and Aries. But it must be mentioned that a reuben, or rube, has been for a long time the term for a back-country hick. Reuben's opponent was usually a Jasper, or city slicker. You could name your twins Reuben and Jasper if you are of a vaudeville turn of mind.

Rex *(Latin)* *"King"*

This is another of those names that goes to Aries, Leo, and Scorpio. One problem, though, is that it also goes to a lot of dogs.

Robert *(Anglo-Saxon)* *"Bright fame"*

This is what Aries and Leo are pulling for. This is a highly popular name, as all the Bobs and Bobbys you can meet every day will testify. Variant forms include Roberto, Rupert, Ruprecht, Rob, Robby, and Robin.

Rodney *(German)* *"Famous"*

Aries and Leo were meant to be celebrities. Rod is the usual nickname form.

Rufus *(Latin) "Red-haired"*

Redheads are believed to be hot, spicy souls, pretty much like Leo, Aries, and Scorpio. Rufus went under a shadow during vaudeville, the way Reuben did. As Rube was the stereotypical hick, Rufe was generally the stereotypical black man. That was a long time ago, however, and the usage seems to have declined. Just as a bit of trivia, Rufus was also the name used by a toy company some years ago for a popular line of stuffed lions.

Samson *(Hebrew) "Resplendent as the sun"*

Well! This would be hard to live up to even without the example of the Biblical Samson. Only a Leo, with its ruler, the sun, can rise to such a challenge. Sam is the pet form, of course. Some people like to spell this Sampson, and as long as it makes them happy, why not?

Waldo *(Anglo-Saxon) "Ruler"*

Leo, Aries, and Scorpio rate this one as well.

VIRGO
the Virgin
August 22 to September 21

Say, you know that stereotypical old maid who bustles about the house with white gloves, checking the picture frames for dust? You probably suspected she belonged under Virgo, but I bet you had the wrong reason.

The Virgo is fastidious, analytical, hypercritical, and precise. She sees everything down to the last detail, and she demands consistency. No one is quite good enough for the Virgo. In fact, she has doubts that even she measures up, but she keeps quiet about them.

A workaholic, Virgo is capable of immense self-denial and labor, though this makes her waspish around people who don't look like they're working as hard as she is. Compliments do not come easily from a Virgo, not only because she is fussy, but because she is one of the least sentimental signs of the Zodiac.

She is slim, graceful, a late bloomer physically, and I bet she has a long nose. She tends toward hypochondria.

But the essence of what you need to know about Virgo is that she is a persnickety old toad, overconcerned with trifles that some people would never...no, I am *not*! Whatever gave you that idea?

Semi-famous Virgos include Robert Benchley, Otto Binder, R. Crumb, Will Cuppy, Carroll John Daly, Roger Duvoisin, John Buchan, C. S. Forester, Walt Kelly, Jack Kirby, Robert McCloskey, Edgar Lee Masters, Bill Nye, Dorothy Parker, Mort Walker, and H. T. Webster.

VIRGO
GIRLS' NAMES

Amelia (Latin) "Industrious, persuasive"

Capricorn and Virgo are industrious enough, but neither is known for being especially persuasive. Gemini and Leo are persuasive but are not as industrious as Virgo. Do what you can with this one. Variant forms of the name include Emily, Amale, Amalia, Amaline, Emmeline, Amelina, Amelinda, and Millie.

Arlene (Celtic) "Pledge"

Virgo, Leo, Scorpio, and Taurus are most likely to keep pledges once they've made them. Virgo will do it because it's the proper thing to do. Some onomasts hold that this is a feminine form of Charles, by way of Charlene, which seems a little far to fetch it. The male form is Arlen. Feminine forms include Arla, Arlette, Arly, Arlana, Arlena, and Arieta.

Aster (Greek) "Star"

The aster is also a flower, considered the birthflower for September. Hence, Virgo. Considered on the "star" meaning alone, it should probably go to Leo or Aries. Variants include Esther, Estelle, Stella, Etoile, Asteria, Aston, Hester, and, simply, Star.

Beverly (Anglo-Saxon) "Beaver meadow"

The beaver maintains its reputation for being a hard-working critter, and is an obvious symbol for Virgo or Capricorn. It has been used for both men and women. Nicknames include Bev, Beaver, and Buffy.

Cecilia (Latin) "Grey-eyed, blind"

Grey, predictably, is the color of Virgo. Alternate forms are Cecile, Cecilie, Cecily, and Sissy. Some onomasts include Celia and Sheila.

VIRGO

Cora *(Greek)* *"Maiden"*

This comes from a Greek goddess known as Kore, about whom not a lot is known. In her day, she made a lot of people uneasy, which certainly sounds like a Virgo. Other forms of the name are Corinne, Corine, Corina, Coretta, Correlle, and Coralie. Corey is sometimes used as a pet form, or nickname.

Cornelia *(Latin)* *"Horn-colored, yellow"*

Most horns that I've seen are more of a bronze shade, but I won't quibble. Yellow is one of Virgo's colors. The masculine form is Cornelius, of course. Nell and Nellie are used as nicknames.

Darla *(Anglo-Saxon)* *"Tenderly beloved"*

Virgos need reassurance occasionally, too. When you're as hypercritical as they are, life gets you down. Darlene is the most common variant, with Daryl and Doralis somewhere behind it. I have never run into anyone named Darling, but I wouldn't put it past some parents.

Deborah *(Hebrew)* *"Bee"*

The bee was, I am told, originally a symbol not just of hard work, but also of wisdom and feminine perfection. Virgo can handle all of that, and she stings, too. There are a lot of different spellings for Deborah, but the most common is Debra. Deb and Debbie are nickname forms.

Fern *(Greek)* *"Fern"*

The fern is considered one of the traditional plants of Virgo. The original Greek word also refers to feathers, so think of light, fragile things.

Giselle *(German)* *"Pledge"*

Taurus, Leo, Virgo, and Scorpio are likely to keep their promises. A colleague has suggested this should go to Virgo because Virgos are always dusting. (I don't think they'll find the body.) Giselle and its variant, Gisella, can be pronounced with a hard G or a soft one. The hard G is the original pronunciation.

VIRGO

Gladys

Well, now, Gladys. Yes. It seems that Gladys is one of those bones of contention that onomasts growl over. One camp says it comes from a Celtic word meaning "princess." Another claims it's just the Welsh feminine form of Claudius, which means "lame, frail, delicate." A third camp says it's the name of a Roman short sword used by gladiators. A fourth says it's a reference to the gladiolus. A few souls make it out as a form of the word "gladness." And one or two people say it was never a real name at all; some novelist just made it up for a book. (Novelists do these things; invented names that have caught on include Pamela and Wendy.)

The biggest groups seem to be the "lame, frail" company and the "gladiolus" battalion. Well, as noted, Virgo leans toward hypochondria, and can be considered frail. And the gladiolus is the flower for August, so Virgo qualifies on both counts. Variants of the name are Glad, Gleda, Gladine, and Gladness.

Grace *(Latin)* *"Grace"*

Gemini, Virgo, and Aquarius are considered the graceful signs. Variants include Gracia, Gracie, and Grazia. Some people also include Griselda. Gracie Allen pulled off the great line about nicknames when she noted, "My real name is Grace, but they call me Gracie for short."

Jane *(Hebrew)* *"God's gracious gift"*

See John, under Aries boys, for details on these "gift" names. Jane is considered a plain name (hence "Plain Jane") and is often beefed up in variants like Janelle, Janine, and Janice. Other forms include Jean, Jeanette, Jeannie, Jan, Janna, Jana, Joan, Joanna, Juana, Juanita, Zinita, Sheena, Shauna, Seana, and Ivana. There are plenty more.

Kanya *(Hindu)* *"Virgin"*

This is another one of those names I slipped in because I ran into it in a name book and liked it. It'll fit in with all the Tanyas and Sonjas in the neighborhood.

Katherine *(Greek)* *"Pure"*

I have been putting Katherine-derived names with signs that are pure something, that is to say, single-minded, or with an obvious overriding characteristic: Aries, Taurus, Cancer, Leo, Virgo, Scorpio, Sagittarius, and Aquarius. But this name has more variant forms than it possibly needs, and there's sure to be a good one for just about any sun sign. Any name that starts with K has a chance of being a Katherine variant, and a lot of C names run the same risk. Some of these include Karen, Karin, Cairn, Karina, Kate, Katie, Katharine, Kathryn, Kathleen, Katrina, Catrina, Catriona, Catalina, Kelly, Kay, Kitty, Kitten, Caitlin, Caitrin, Caron, Cass, Catharine, Ekaterina, Kass, Catherine, Katushka, Kathy, Cathy, Trina, Cath, Cat and on and on and on and on.

Laura *(Latin) "Laurel"*

The laurel wreath is a crown sought after by Leo, Aries, and Scorpio, and occasionally achieved by the overachievers Virgo and Capricorn. The masculine forms start with Lawrence, of course. Feminine forms include Laure, Laurie, Lori, Laurette, Lara, Laurencia, Larunda, Laurel, and Loretta.

Leah *(Hebrew) "Weary"*

This is obviously for the hardworking Virgos and Capricorns. Variant forms are hard to tell, since they mix in with so many of the variants of Leo (lion) and Leigh (meadow). Leah can pronounced with one syllable or two. My feeling is that if you're going to pronounce it with one, you might as well use Lee and be done with it. (Many people have a tendency to pronounce Leigh to rhyme with May. It's a nervous reaction to fancy spelling.)

Leda *(Greek) "Lady"*

This refers to the lady of the house, which is a job Virgo can handle, but also has a touch of sin, since the original Leda is not known for being a lady. This might give a Virgo a new outlook on things. Lida is a variant.

Lily *(Latin) "Lily"*

The lily is a sign of perfection, that all-consuming ideal of Virgo. Trying to improve a lily, "gilding a lily," is a byword for foolishly trying to improve something that doesn't need it. And that's occasionally a trait of Virgo as well. Forms of the name include Lil, Lilice, Lilian, Lillian, Lillie, Lili, Lilias, and Liuka.

VIRGO

Melissa *(Greek) "Honeybee"*

This is another symbol for the workaholics of the Zodiac, Virgo and Capricorn. Melita, Lissa, and Missy are variant forms.

Monique *(Italian) "Advisor"*

Like Mona, this also has a secondary meaning of "one" or "unique," but this doesn't seem to have a lot to do with the advice. Leo, Virgo, and Capricorn are always giving advice, and some of it must be unique. They are also the sorts who will be around to say "I told you so" if you don't take the advice. Moni, Mona, and Monica are variant forms.

Nora *(Latin) "Honor"*

This is obviously short for Honora, the original form of the name. Leo, Scorpio, and Virgo are strong on personal honor. This name is also short for just about any other name ending in "nor," to the point that some onomasts don't think it's a separate name at all.

Octavia *(Latin) "Eighth"*

The masculine form is Octavius, of course. Either can be applied to the eighth month, in which case it falls to Leo and Virgo, or to the eighth sign of the Zodiac, Scorpio.

Penelope *(Greek) "Weaver"*

The original Penelope, trying to avoid a dangerous decision, promised everyone she would decide as soon as she finished this last little bit of weaving she had to do. Every night, she would sneak out and unweave what she had laboriously woven during the day. She apparently kept this up for a couple of decades, but instead of becoming a symbol of procrastination, became a byword for industriousness and faithfulness. This makes it a fine name for Virgo. The pet form is Penny.

Sabrina *(Anglo-Saxon?) "Princess"*

The onomasts are far from clear on this. They seem to suggest that Sabrina was an Anglo-Saxon princess after whom the Roman conquerors, for some reason, named the Severn River. This seems a little dubious, since the Anglo-Saxons didn't make it into England until after the Romans had left. Maybe it's an Anglo-Saxon princess who was named after the Severn River. And whatever she did to become famous, she doesn't seem to have gotten much reward for it, outside of having other girls named after her; at least, no one seems to recall what it was. Virgo is the type to work away at something without getting much credit, and until someone explains Sabrina better, I will leave her here. There was one attempt to make it a form of Sabra, which refers to a small cactus or a native of Israel. But that hardly explains the Severn River. I don't know if any Anglophile has ever named children Sabrina and Thomas, for the Severn and the Thames, but it's always a possibility.

Sapphire *(Greek)* *"Sapphire"*

This is the birthstone for September, covering Virgo and Libra; its main power is to safeguard mental and moral safety. One can always use a little help there. Sapphira is a popular version.

Susan *(Hebrew)* *"Lily"*

See Lily, above. The lily is also a symbol of Spring, of Easter, and of the Virgin Mary, though I would like it made clear she is not the virgin referred to in the Zodiac. Variants of Susan are popular and all over the place, including Sue, Suzy, Susie, Susanne, Susanna, Suzette, Sukey, and Zsa Zsa.

Virginia *(Latin)* *"Virginal"*

Well, just guess. Ginny and Ginger are frequent nickname forms.

Wilhemina *(German)* *"Will helmet"*

A helmet of will power, you see. It is a name for someone with great will, drive, and ability. Scorpio, Aries, Virgo, and Capricorn are the self-propelled signs of the Zodiac. The male form is William, of course. Variant and nickname forms for girls include Wilma, Velma, Mina, Minnie, Wilmette, Elma, Mimi, Willie, Billie, and Guglielma.

Winona *(American Indian) "Eldest daughter"*

The oldest member of the family gets a reputation for watching over the younger ones, whether the younger ones want to be watched over or not. Parents, as they get older, may relax rules with the younger siblings, but the older ones remember the old rules and look on with disapproval. Sound like Virgo to you? Wenona and Winonah are variants.

VIRGO
BOYS' NAMES

Adam *(Hebrew) "Man of red earth"*

This would fit nicely on one of the earth signs: Taurus, Virgo, or Capricorn. Any of the three would also be able to live with the penalty Adam suffered, being condemned to live by the sweat of his brow.

Ambrose *(Greek) "Immortal, divine"*

This is the sort of thing Capricorn and Virgo are always shooting for, but Aries, Leo, and Scorpio always get.

Amos *(Hebrew) "Burden"*

Capricorn and Virgo are the type to shoulder burdens. Mind you, they always think they're carrying more than they actually are. But they do take on more than enough.

Barclay *(Anglo-Saxon) "Birch meadow"*

Birch is one of the highly prized woods that has dozens of uses, from furniture to canoe skins to tanning (leather or children). It would obviously be best applied to the competent and the versatile: Aquarius, Virgo, or Gemini. A variant spelling is Berkeley. Pet forms are Barc and Bic.

Casper *(Persian) "Treasure keeper"*

Taurus and Cancer are the keepers and defenders of the Zodiac. Virgo would make a good treasurer, too; someone has to keep accounts straight. Variant forms of this are Jasper, Caspar, and Gaspar. Cass is a nickname form.

Christopher *(Greek) "Christ-bearer"*

The original Christopher, according to legend, carried a child across a stream, only to have the boy get heavier and heavier. He eventually learned he had been carrying a vision of Christ and was granted a hint of what it felt like to have the whole world's sins on his shoulders. Virgo and Capricorn, as noted, are the burden-carriers. There are numerous variants and pet forms, including Cristobal, Christophe, Kester, Krzysztof, Chris, and Kit.

Colin *(Gaelic) "Child"*

This name is obviously related to Colleen. It belongs to the young-looking people, generally the ones born under Gemini, Virgo, or Capricorn.

Conan *(Celtic) "Wisdom"*

Where you put a name like this depends on your perception of wisdom. If you like common sense, Aries, Taurus, and Virgo are the ones to choose. The name has gotten a push lately from the resurgence of interest in the tales of Conan the Barbarian. Conan was more of a Scorpio, though: always brooding. Variant forms are Kynan and Conant.

Cosmo *(Greek) "Order, universe"*

A cosmologist is someone who tries to understand the essential order of the universe. Noncosmologists say this is difficult because there is no essential order to the universe. Virgo is more the cosmologist type. Cosimo is a variant spelling.

Calvin *(Latin) "Bald"*

Actually, most Calvins are named either for John Calvin, the early Protestant, or for Calvin Coolidge, President of the United States. Both were known as fairly dry, persnickety men. Cal is the pet form.

Elias *(Hebrew) "Jehovah is Lord"*

Scorpio and Taurus are the most firm in their religious beliefs. Virgo would like to be; maybe this would help. Variants are Eli, Elijah, Ellis, Elliott, and Elihu. You don't see many Elihus these days, except among very loyal Yale alumni.

Emery *(German) "Industrious"*

Virgo and Capricorn, as noted, are the hard-working signs in the Zodiac. Variants are Amery, Emmerick, Amerigo, Imre, and Emory.

Floyd *(Celtic) "Grey"*

This is a color of Gemini and a color of Virgo. None of the onomasts I saw would explain why Lloyd and Floyd should both mean the same thing, and none that I noticed said one was a form of the other. You may flip a coin.

Gary *(German) "Spear carrier"*

You may consider this another warrior sign. A spear carrier these days is also known as an extra, a supernumerary, someone who doesn't do anything very flashy or exciting, but is needed on hand to do a little work and fill in your numbers. Virgo and Capricorn get these kinds of dull jobs all the time. Gary is also used as a short form for Garrett or Garrison.

Gilbert *(German) "Illustrious pledge"*

The pledge keepers are Virgo, Taurus, Leo, and Scorpio. Wilbert and Wilbur are sometimes considered variants. Gil and sometimes Gillie are pet forms.

Graham *(Anglo-Saxon) "Grey home"*

Virgo is likely to have a grey home, not only becase grey is Virgo's color, but because he very likely keeps the shades drawn so the sun doesn't fade the furniture. Graeme and Gram are variants.

Horatio *(Latin) "Time keeper"*

Virgo would keep meticulous records, and will probably keep the clock running right to the second, as well. There used to be plenty of Horatios back in the ways when children were expected to memorize the heroic tale "Horatius at the Bridge." We no longer demand these things, feeling the children will turn out better without it. The report on results is not yet in. A variant form of Horatio is Horace.

Jeremiah *(Hebrew) "Appointed by Jehovah"*

Scorpio, Leo, and Aries will believe this. Virgo will act as if he believed it. Jeremy, Jerrold, and Jerry are variants.

Julius *(Latin) "Youthful looking"*

Literally, this means someone who has a very light, downy beard or mustache. Gemini, Virgo, and Capricorn are the signs that stay young-looking the longest, though I can't vouch for the beard. Jules and Giles are variants. Julie is generally used as the nickname.

Lance *(German) "Land"*

This ought to go to an earth sign: Taurus, Virgo, or Capricorn. It is also short for Lancelot, whose standards were almost as high as Virgo's. Lancelot apparently means "servant."

Lester *(Latin) "Camp of the Legion"*

Wherever the Roman Legions stopped, they had to make camp, setting it up according to very strict rules regarding arrangement, situation, and structure. This is obviously the sort of thing Virgos would go for. Leicester is a variant, and probably the original.

Mahlon *(Hebrew) "Sick person"*

This is a good choice if you want to sympathize with Virgo's hypochondria.

Malcolm *(Gaelic) "Servant of St. Columba"*

Cancer, Capricorn, Libra, Pisces, and Virgo would make good followers or servants. Virgo would be especially good. He would anticipate every requirement and be ready with it when it was needed.

VIRGO

Meredith *(Welsh)* *"Protector from the sea"*

You'll have to do some of your own interpretation here. If this means a protector who comes from the sea, give it to a water sign: Cancer, Pisces, or Scorpio. But if you think it represents a dam or some other kind of earthworks put up to protect people from the sea, give it to an earth sign, like Virgo, Taurus, or Capricorn.

Seth *(Hebrew)* *"Compensation"*

Capricorn, Cancer, Scorpio, and Virgo always feel they require compensation for something. Virgo, in addition, is always trying to compensate for what he sees as his own shortcomings.

Sherlock *(Anglo-Saxon)* *"Fair hair"*

Okay, now you know that. Now forget it. Anyone named Sherlock is obviously named for Sherlock Holmes, who is a Virgo character if ever I saw one. Sherlockians give his birthdate as January 6, 1854, but I haven't seen a birth certificate yet. (Considering this was in the Victorian era, you don't suppose this is one of those cases where the birth was postdated to...er...avoid embarrassing questions, do you?)

Stuart *(Anglo-Saxon)* *"Steward"*

If you think a steward is a servant, give the name to Virgo or Capricorn. If you think of a steward as one who takes care of someone else's property, make it Taurus or Cancer. Stu is the common pet form.

Sven *(Scandinavian)* *"Youth"*

The young-looking signs are, as mentioned, Virgo, Capricorn, and Gemini. Swen is a variant.

Wayne *(Anglo-Saxon)* *"Waggoner"*

That is, someone who drives a wagon. Once upon a time, these men had to load the wagon themselves, unload, and be prepared to account for everything in the load. This makes it a Virgo job.

LIBRA

the Scales

September 22 to October 21

Some people call Libra the best-looking sign of the Zodiac, while others say Libra's all right if you like that type. Libra tends toward curves, dimples, bow-shaped little mouths, and precious features.

The disposition that goes with that is pretty much what you'd expect. Libras are sweet and a bit naive. They abhor a fuss and they never like to make a decision until they've heard all sides of the question. Libra is eager to please, and thus easily bulldozed. Desiring justice and harmony above everything, the average Libra is the sort of person who says, "Well, I just don't know," and "There's a lot to be said on both sides," and "It's difficult to know what to do." If possible, Libra will sit back and wait, hoping that if the decision is postponed long enough, things will take care of themselves.

Libra is charming but unstable; being pinned down to anything is abhorrent. Libras are good with children and have nice, gentle voices. Many have creative impulses, but never get around to doing anything about these.

Libras are nice to have around, if you're not in a hurry.

Semi-famous Libra characters include Al Capp, Elizabeth Daly, Annie Fanny, Stuart Kaminsky, Lily Langtry, Robert Lawson, Elmore Leonard, Lois Lenski, Damon Runyon, Frank Sullivan, and Kate Douglass Wiggin.

LIBRA
GIRLS' NAMES

Autumn *(English)* *"Autumn"*

This is simple enough, a name for Libra, Scorpio, or Sagittarius. Fall is not an acceptable substitute.

Beatrice *(Latin)* *"She who makes happy"*

Libra is always eager to please. There are many variants of the name: Beatrix, Bea, Trixie, Tricia, and Bebe.

Bunny *(English)* *"Bunny"*

This is a sweet, cuddly name, for Libra or Pisces. Rabbit and Hare do not have the same effect.

Calliope *(Greek)* *"Beautiful voice"*

I swear I'm not making that up. Libra is supposed to have the prettiest voice in the Zodiac. Ordinarily, I wouldn't have mentioned the name at all, but I am told that "Days of Our Lives" has been responsible for bringing it back into vogue. Soaps and romance novels have an inevitable effect, it seems, on children's names. Some people should not be allowed any type of reading at all until after the child is safely christened. We have not found out to this day where my Great-aunt Birdeva's name came from, but we suspect her mother's mother, who, in her own day, had been responsible for the name Glennorah. See what I mean?

Carmel *(Hebrew)* *"Garden"*

This is a calm, peaceful place for Taurus, Libra, or Cancer. Since the word "caramel" is frequently pronounced like Carmel, you get an added sweetness that applies to Libra. Variants are Carmella, Carmilla, Carmetta, and sometimes Carmen. Carmiel is sometimes considered a variant, though other experts say this is a separate name, meaning "Garden of the Lord."

LIBRA

Carmen *(Latin)* *"Song"*

This can be considered another tribute to Libra's voice. Of course, the original Carmen, the cigarette roller who vamped bullfighters, was more of a Scorpio, or perhaps a Capricorn. This is not brought up in the opera.

Charity *(English)* *"Charity"*

Libra is always willing to give people things, especially the benefit of the doubt. Cherry and Charis are considered separate names by some, and forms of Charity by others.

Edith *(German)* *"Rich gift"*

See John, under Aries boys, for details on "gift" names. Variants of the name include Eda, Edie, Edyth, and Editha.

Erin *(Gaelic)* *'Peace"*

This is obviously an Irish form of Irene. It is also used as a synonym for Ireland. I have a feeling there are things to be said about referring to Ireland by a name that means "peace," but I value my health. Many people prefer Erin to Erica as a feminine form of Eric, and I suspect that's behind its recent surge in popularity. Erina is sometimes used, as well.

Fiona *(Celtic)* *"White, fair"*

Fair means both light-complected and good-looking, primarily because our ancestors believed that to be truly beautiful you had to be both pale and blonde. In fact, it became a common compliment among some poets to refer to a woman as blonde, no matter what her hair color was, to imply that she was remarkably good-looking. A lot of our lore about blondes would not exist at all if the poets had been a little bit brighter. But then they wouldn't have been poets, I suppose. At any rate, this name can be another tribute to Libra's good looks. It is favored in soaps and romances because it has a tinge of the wild and the Celtic. Some people prefer the form Viona.

Frieda *(German)* *"Peaceful"*

This is a short form for Frederica, another one of those names that is fading away because it's too long to say in the MTV age. The long form was always a problem anyway because people could never decide whether to pronounce it Fredder-eeka or Fred-Erica. Other forms are Freda and Frida.

Honey *(English) "Honey"*

Honey is sweet and generally good for you, and so is Libra. Some people consider Honi to be a variant, though others make it a separate name, meaning "gracious" in Hebrew.

Irene *(Greek) "Peace"*

This is another name obviously meant for Libra, and the only problem with it is that so many people want to play with the spelling. You may have Eirene, Irina, Irini, Ireen, and Irinna, not to mention Ira, Rini, Rina, Rena, and Erin. This is one of the drawbacks of living in a country where you don't have to okay your baby's name with the government before you use it. (There are such places. And you thought having to wear a seat belt was a restriction of your liberty.)

Isadora *(Latin) "Gift of Isis"*

The people who know these things make Isis the Egyptian version of Venus, or Aphrodite, who rules Libra.

Jade *(French/Spanish) "Jade"*

Jade has been a prized stone for centuries, and endowed with all kinds of mystic powers. The Chinese consider jade to be the concentrated essence of love, which would obviously appeal to Libra. I'm not sure what all this has to do with the fact that jade, as a slang expression, refers to a woman of uncertain morals. Furthermore, if you have been indulging in sensational things long enough, so that you are unlikely to be shocked or even interested any more, you are said to be jaded. What about that, eh? My own feeling is that you should stick to the concentrated essence of love; the Chinese were there first, after all.

Jewel *(English) "Jewel"*

Libras tend to be sweet, precious souls, and this suits them. Jewell and Joya are sometimes used as variants. The French form, Bijou, is also considered a cute name, although it suffers in this country from all the movie theaters by that name. On the other hand, if her parents met in a theater, this is a better choice for a name than, say, "Highway 44 Elite Drive-In."

Lace *(English)* *"Lace"*

Lace is considered light, frilly, and feminine, and that is how Libra girls are often considered, too. I might point out that good lace, though it looks frothy and light, requires hours of painstaking effort to look that way. No further comment is necessary. Layce is a variant.

Lila *(Hebrew)* *"Delicate"*

Actually, this is a short form of Delilah, for which you should check under Scorpio girls. But Delilah achieved something of a reputation, and this form achieved major use as an independent name.

Linda *(Spanish)* *"Beautiful"*

The onomasts grudgingly accept this, though they prefer to attribute mystic meanings to anything with "lind" in it. Pisces, Scorpio, and Libra are supposed to be among the best-looking of signs, though I like to think the rest of us aren't too bad, either. Lindy and Lindie are common nicknames.

Lulu *(Anglo-Saxon)* *"Soothing influence"*

Actually, the onomasts have been tussling over this. Some claim it comes from an American Indian word meaning "rabbit," while others sneer that it's just baby talk for Lucy, or Louise. Still, for the soothing influence, which is the majority opinion, it ought to go to Libra. Luckily, Libra has this thing for rabbits, and, well, baby talk is no problem for her, either.

Melody *(English)* *"Melody"*

This is another name honoring the vocal qualities of Libra. Mel and Melly are nicknames, though Melly will suffer all her life from people who think it's Nelly.

LIBRA

Miel (French) "Honey"

Libra's sweetness is pointed up again in this name. A few experts make it a feminine form of Mihiel, the French form of Michael.

Mildred (Anglo-Saxon) "Mild speech, mild advice"

This name seems to suggest Libra's generally peaceable qualities. It is considered something of an old-fashioned name, and has fallen out of favor except as applied to old maids, nosy neighbors, and annoying children in sitcoms. But it may yet recover. Millie is the nickname form.

Olivia (Latin) "Olive"

Here is another symbol of peace, Libra's great goal. The basic name Olive is not as popular as the variants, which include Olivette, Livy, and Livia.

Pamela (Greek) "All-honey"

This sweet name was apparently made up by Sir Phillip Sidney in the sixteenth century and was popularized by Samuel Richardson in the eighteenth, when he made Pamela the star of what is considered one of the first novels in the English language. Pamelina is used as a variant by people who just have to be that way. Pam is the pet form.

Sarah (Hebrew) "Princess"

Despite all the stories in the tabloids, "princess" still implies to most people a sweet, refined girl who wears glass slippers, lives in a palace, and eventually marries charming Prince Charming, a gent with wavy blond hair and a dimple in his chin. This might very well be true. Heaven knows I've never believed everything I read in the tabloids, and I don't know any princesses personally. Anyway, it all sounds like the kind of life a Leo or a Libra would enjoy. There are plenty of variant forms of the name: Sarey, Sara, Sarita, Sadie, Shari, Sharon, and Sally.

Velvet (English) "Velvet"

This goes to Libra because it is soft and luxurious. A hyper-fancy form is Velouette.

Wendy

Well, no one's quite sure about this. Most onomasts think James M. Barrie just made it up for a book he originally called *Peter Pan and Wendy*. But then they go on to try to figure out how he made up the name. Did he get it from Gwendolyn? Or did he just go back to childhood baby talk for the term "friendy-wendy"? Well, Gwendolyn means someone fair of face, and Libra is certainly a friendy-wendy to those she meets, so the name seems to fit here, no matter where it came from.

Winifred *(German)* *"Friend of peace"*

This is another name that obviously belongs to Libra. Winnie, Freddy, Una, and Oona are variant forms.

Winsome *(English)* *"Winsome"*

The word winsome doesn't get a lot of use these days, but it means cute. Or, rather, it's the word we used to use before cute took over. It seems that the use of the word cute to mean something small, adorable, or winsome, is an American slang use that proper word experts despise. Cute was originally meant as a short form of acute, and meant something precise. From there it became an adjective for anything well done, and from there it rolled on to a thousand different meanings: winsome, foolish, small, clever, disgusting, pretty, and overly sweet, to name but a few. Winsome escaped all this by becoming obsolete, and it is perfectly safe now as a name for Libra, who can be cute in many ways and meanings. Winnie is the natural nickname form.

LIBRA
BOYS' NAMES

Beau *(French)* *"Handsome"*

Libra, Scorpio, and Pisces are considered some of the best-looking signs in the Zodiac. The name has also benefited from the recent trend toward short, sharp names, especially in the form Bo. This was once a slang term for a bum, or hobo. Only in America.

Bradford *(Anglo-Saxon)* *"Broad ford"*

A broad ford means a nice, easy crossing, the sort of thing Libra appreciates. Pet forms are Brad and Ford.

Busby *(Scottish)* *"Village in the woods"*

This sounds like a remote sort of place, quiet, slow, relatively peaceful: the kind of place Libra, Cancer, Pisces, and Taurus would shine in. Buzz is the nickname.

Chester *(Latin)* *"Fortress"*

Cancer and Taurus are the types likely to *act* like fortresses; Cancer, Libra, and Pisces are the kinds who would like to *hide* inside them. Chet is the usual nickname form.

Clement *(Latin)* *"Merciful"*

Libra, Sagittarius, Pisces, and Aquarius tend toward mercy. The pet form, Clem, is considered another backwoods, rube sort of name. Variant forms are Clemence, Clemens, and Kelmen. The feminine form is Clementine.

Corey *(Gaelic)* *"Dweller in a ravine"*

This sounds like another hiding place for Libra, Cancer, and Pisces. It is frequently applied to girls, but is not really considered a form of the name Cora.

Crispin *(Latin)* *"Curly"*

Libra and Taurus are the signs most likely to have naturally curly hair.

Cyprian *(Latin)* *"One from Cyprus"*

And Cyprus is known for its copper. But this is beside the point. Cyprus is where Aphrodite, goddess of love, was born, more or less, and one of her titles was Cyprian. All of Aphrodite's titles were, at one time or another, used as slang expressions for prostitutes. Aphrodite, if such a person actually existed, seems to have been something of a Libra character herself, though, as Venus, she rules both Libra and Taurus. This name has been used for both boys and girls.

Dale *(Norse) "Valley"*

This is another hiding place for those who want peace—Pisces, Libra, and Cancer. Both boys and girls are named Dale.

Ellery *(German) "Alder tree"*

Alder, sometimes known as elder, is a tree known for its soft, manageable wood. Libra is soft and manageable, too.

Elmo *(Greek) "Amiable"*

That's Libra down to the ground. This name has been growing a little in popularity since a character named Elmo joined the cast of "Sesame Street."

Eustace *(Greek) "Fruitful"*

This is the sort of thing for spring, or for harvest time. So give it to Aries, Taurus, Libra, or Scorpio. Eustacia is sometimes given to girls; Stacey is used for either sex.

Frederick *(German) "Peaceful ruler"*

Taurus and Libra are the most likely types to rule in a calm, peaceful manner. Friedrich, Freddy, Fred, and Fritz are variants. A few people, agreeing with Peter Sellers that Fred is basically a funny name, have tried Phred and Pfred. This made it less silly?

Geoffrey *(German) "God's peace"*

This is a form of Godfrey, and is obviously meant for the peaceful signs of Libra, Cancer, and Taurus. Geoffrey is the form preferred in England (where they still spell "jail" gaol.) Jeffrey is the preferred form here. The pet form is Jeff over here, Geoff across the ocean.

Howland *(Anglo-Saxon) "Hilly land"*

You may interpret this as an area of rough terrain, in which case it might be best for Sagittarius or Scorpio. Or you can think of it as a series of gentle curves, in which case it fits Libra best.

Hugo *(German)* *"Heart, mind"*

Libra and Pisces have both of these, and to spare. Hugh is another form.

Humphrey *(German)* *"Peace monger"*

Most of the onomasts make this "supporter of peace" or "guardian of peace"; others differ, but all seem to feel peace has something to do with it. Peace in any form is Libra's prime objective.

Jonah *(Hebrew)* *"Dove"*

Well, the dove is a symbol of peace, so this has been given to Libra. Jonah, used as a noun, is a symbol of bad luck, though, so perhaps Capricorn is the place for this. Jonah himself seems to have been a Scorpio character.

Junior *(English)* *"Junior"*

This is an all-purpose diminutive. A lot of children would resent it, but Libra, Cancer, and Pisces would be the least likely to do so.

Justin *(Latin)* *"Just"*

Libra and the scales are symbols of justice, and Libra is very concerned about it. This is one reason Libra likes peace; it provides enough time to judge, to hear all sides of the question, before coming to a decision. Justis, Justus, and Justinian are variants. Justine is the feminine form.

Lee *(Anglo-Saxon)* *"Meadow"*

This seems a nice, peaceful place for Taurus, Cancer, and Libra. Lee can also be considered short for Libra, if you're that hard up for justification. It is also spelled Leigh, and can be given to boys or to girls.

Lyman *(Anglo-Saxon)* *"Valley"*

This is another sheltered place for the Libra, Cancer, or Pisces. You can use Manny for a pet form.

Manfred (German) "Man of peace"

This sounds like Libra again. Both Manny and Fred are used as pet forms.

Myron (Greek) "Fragrant ointment"

Myrrh, to be exact. Libra is the type to be interested in something this luxurious. If you prefer to think of myrrh as an exotic commodity, carried over long distances from strange lands, then Gemini and Aquarius are the right places for it.

Oliver (Latin) "Olive"

The olive branch is as traditional a sign of peace as the dove, and is thus appropriate to Libra. Ollie, Ole, and Olivier are variant forms.

Simon (Greek) "He who hears"

Gemini gets marks for hearing everything exciting there is to hear, but for a good listener, you must go to Libra, Cancer, Taurus, and Pisces. They're the ones who will listen as long as you want to talk. Si and Simeon are variants.

Solomon (Hebrew) "Peaceful"

This is Libra's, naturally. Solomon is also a symbol of wisdom and justice, which also concern Libra. Suleiman is a variant; so is Shlomo.

Tobias (Hebrew) "The Lord is good"

The optimism of this is worthy of Leo or Libra. Tobin and Tobit are variants; Toby is the pet form. Toby, in fact, is far more popular than any of the longer forms.

Trevor (Celtic) "Prudent"

Taurus, Capricorn, and Libra are very prudent. If Libra were any more prudent, he'd be virtually motionless. The name does not have a very large following, despite Trevor Howard. Some people pronounce it with a short e, and some with a long. Variants are Trefor, Trev, and Truver.

Vladimir *(Russian/Slavic) "Ruling world, possessing peace"*

This is another name for Libra. It is fairly unusual in this country, but there's one nice thing about an unusual name: Miss Chickee on Romper Room never peeks at you through that magic mirror. Vladimir can be pronounced as it is spelled, but the experts pronounce it Vlad-yee-myeer. Vlad and Vadim are short forms.

SCORPIO
the Scorpion
October 22 to November 21

Scorpios should go back to the soaps and romances, where they belong. They can be much too exhausting in real life.

Have you read about those heroes with deep, intense eyes that burn with inner fire? The characters with secret passions and hidden pasts? Immense drive and compelling animal magnetism? Scorpios, every one of them.

With their intense drive and natural dignity, Scorpios are often mistaken for superior beings by less single-minded folk. The Scorpios often believe it themselves. They love to prove their superiority, accepting any challenge, particularly one involving great physical exertion. They have a moderate tendency to prey on those they perceive as weaker than themselves. But they will never make much money; they prefer to spend it.

Perceptive, brave, and true, they make constant friends. They also make constant enemies, and you might not know which you are until it's too late. They are as subtle as they are deep, brooding in silence over real or imagined slights. They are uncommonly suspicious and have violent tempers.

Some astrologers divide all Scorpios into two groups: those who emulate the scorpion (the bad guys) and those who emulate the eagle, another symbol of the sign. I wish you many of the latter.

Semi-famous Scorpios include Alistair Cooke, Steve Ditko, Chester Gould, William Hope Hodgson, Arthur Guiterman, Emily Kimbrough, Bill Mauldin, Burton Rascoe, Kate Seredy, William Steig, Vincent Starrett, Bert Leston Taylor, and Chauncey B. Tinker. James Bond was probably a Scorpio. Rhett Butler was a Scorpio with a Sagittarius influence.

SCORPIO
GIRLS' NAMES

Alva *(Latin)* *"White"*

There seems to be an added connotation of brightness. Scorpio, like Aries, burns with a white heat, even though Scorpio is a water sign. Variants are Alvah and Albina. It is also sometimes used as a feminine form of Alvin.

Arwen *(English)*

I was a little surprised to find that J. R. R. Tolkien seems to have made this up for one of his heroines. It sounded like a perfectly ordinary name to me, until I started to look it up. According to Tolkien, the name is an Elvish word meaning "Royal Maiden," and is thus just the sort of thing for Aries, Leo, and Scorpio, the aristocrats of the Zodiac.

Dahlia *(English)* *"Dahlia"*

This is a flower name, but it carries exotic implications and is considered a little sinister. There is the Black Dahlia, one of the most brutal unsolved murders on the books. Then there was the *Blue Dahlia*, a famous mystery movie. (In the original version, the best friend did it, but they were forced to change the ending to make it more cheerful.) Maybe dahlias are all right, and it's only the black and blue ones you have to watch out for. But I'm going to play it safe and give the name to Scorpio, who commonly carries an air of exotic menace about her.

Daphne *(Greek)* *"Laurel"*

This is another crown name for Aries, Scorpio, and Leo, as you will recall from the use of laurel wreaths as signs of victory in Classical Greece. This was begun as a memorial by Apollo to Daphne, who, rather than go out with him (if you know what I mean), had herself turned into a tree. Using her leaves as a wreath given to winners of the highest honors was meant to be Apollo's way of being apologetic, say the experts. I doubt it. He probably thought it was a pretty clever joke to get some use out of her. Apollo was like that. Just to lower the intellectual level of this paragraph, I will mention that the nickname form is Daffy.

SCORPIO

Delilah *(Hebrew)* *"Delicate"*

The onomasts aren't quite sure about this. Others say it means "languishing" or "pining with desire." The problem is, of course, that for most of us there is just one Delilah: the hardboiled young lady who vamped Samson. So if you want to give this name to someone delicate, try Virgo or Pisces. Libra may languish. But for the woman who knows what she wants and doesn't care how she gets it, go to Scorpio or Aries.

Desire *(English)* *"Desire"*

Scorpios are frequently consumed with desire. The French form, Desirée, is a little more popular, as it denotes a woman who is desired rather than one who does the desiring herself.

Erma *(German)*

The onomasts have the most trouble with these short, simple names. They can't decide whether it is a form of Emma, of Hermione, of Ermine, of Irmintrude, or of half a dozen other possibilities. The majority make it out to mean something like "royal" or "noble," and it is thus another name for Aries, Leo, and Scorpio, the aristocrats. Irma was once the preferred form, but Erma has eclipsed it, probably assisted by Erma Bombeck.

Erna *(German)* *"Earnest"*

One who is earnest is serious about her goals. This is certainly a Scorpio. A number of onomasts differ, though, deriving it from the Anglo-Saxon word for "eagle." This is also a Scorpio attribute.

Hope *(Anglo-Saxon)* *"Hope"*

Leo, Libra, and Pisces are the most optimistic signs. But it might help out the gloom merchants, Scorpio and Capricorn, if you laid this on them. In addition, see Opal, in this section.

Kelly *(Gaelic)* *"Warlike woman"*

The fiercest women seem to be the Arians and the Scorpios. You used to have to be Irish to get away with a first name like Kelly, and probably red-haired. But this is a free country, and now anyone can get in on it.

Some people say Kelly is a form of Katherine, and others derive it from Kelilah. There are also arguments concerning Kiley and Keely. Kelley, at any rate, is a variant.

Layla *(Arabic) "Night"*

The experts tell me this means "dark as night" and was used to symbolize everything the Arabs wanted in a woman: dark hair, large dark eyes, a humble demeanor, complete dependence on and subservience to her husband, and so on. (A book called *The Perfumed Garden* spells it out, one might say, to the last detail.) Around these parts, however, the name is considered exotic, and symbolizes dark-eyed, seething women, the sort Scorpio is supposed to produce. Laila, Leila, and Lela are variants, and sometimes Lila is used as well. The onomasts do not seem to see any connection between this name and Delilah, so I suppose it's silly of me to even bring it up.

Lilith *(Hebrew)*

No one's sure what this means, except that it implies something dark and nasty that lurks in shadows. According to folklore, Lilith was Adam's first wife. She was thrown out of the garden for being a troublemaker and was replaced by Eve. She grew up to be the mother of all vampires, evil spirits, and other monsters who prey on the children of Eve. Let's be charitable and say she was a woman with an intense drive toward certain career goals and a tendency to nurse a grudge. This sounds like Scorpio again. Lillith and Lilliz are variants.

Lindsey *(German)*

This is some kind of island, agree the experts, but you'll notice it has "lind" in it, so they haven't decided what kind of island yet. It involves linden trees, or snakes, or both. Scorpio is inclined to try to be an island, despite the poem. The name can also be spelled Lindsay, and is given to boys and to girls.

Lobelia *(English) "Lobelia"*

I thought this flower name would present no problems, but it seems to be another name that J. R. R. Tolkien sneaked past me; the onomasts don't want to list it. As mentioned before, most flower names have been used as girl's names, with the exception of maybe snapdragon or Dutchman's breeches. In checking on flower names, I consulted a number of those fine old Victorian books on the meanings of the flowers. But this is a much less exact science than astrology or onomastics. I don't want to say that these dear old souls just put down anything they liked for the meaning of each flower, but unless someone rushes me evidence to the contrary, I may have to. Anyhow, all the flower books I checked indicated that there was something menacing about lobelias. And Tolkien gave the name to a particularly pushy Hobbit. Lobelia Sackville-Baggins probably had more than a little Scorpio in her.

Lorelei *(German) "Alluring one"*

I'm going to get into trouble; I just know it. Other signs get nice names, like Ruth, or Ruby, or Greta. But for Scorpio I have collected a rogue's gallery. The lorelei were German mermaids, lovely ladies who tempted sailors to their doom. They were pretty and perilous, as Scorpios are inclined to be. Variants include Lurlene, Lurleen, Lurette, Lura, Lorilee, and Allura.

Lynn *(Anglo-Saxon) "Cascade"*

You may put this name where you like, depending on how hard you think the water is falling in this cascade. Scorpio seems to suggest an irresistible rush. Linn and Lynette are common variants. All these are also used as pet names for Adeline, Linda, Belinda, Melinda, and so on. Lynn is one of the most common name elements for tacking onto the end of another element to make a new name, as in Marylinn or Laurelin. I tried for years to get someone to try Amandalin, but I have just about given up.

Mary *(Hebrew) "Bitter, rebellious"*

See Miriam, under Cancer girls, for notes on this name. As mentioned there, the meaning will do for Scorpio, but the name is far too traditional. Still, there are so many variant forms that you ought to be able to find one or two to fit. Some more, not mentioned under Miriam, are Marion, Marian, Mirham, Mitzi, Mitsy, Mariel, Marielle, Marriette, Marushka, Merrilee, Merry, Meryl, Meriel, Muriel, Molly, Mollie, Moira, Maureen, and so on. There are probably enough variants for everyone, no matter what their sun sign.

SCORPIO

Maureen *(Latin) "Dark"*

Not everyone agrees that Maureen is a form of Mary, above. Scorpio is inclined to be both dark and bitter, though, so it would fit here nicely. To some people, Maureen suggests a more open, outdoorsy type (see the book *How Not to Name the Baby*), and it might fit a Sagittarius better if you're of that mind. Moreen and Maurine are variants; Morris is the masculine form.

Maxine *(Latin) "The greatest"*

This is another name for the Aries, Leo, and Scorpio types, the strivers.

Moira *(Celtic) "Great"*

Some people think this is a form of Mary, too. Scorpio can be either great or bitter, and sometimes both.

Opal *(Sanskrit) "Opal"*

The opal is a symbol of hope. It is also the birthstone for September, which puts it in the Libra and Scorpio zone. But opals, particularly black opals, are considered omens of bad luck, talismans of sinister forces. Scorpio won't mind that. There is a small core of people who, every year, insist the black opal is pretty and demand it for their wedding or engagement rings. They can't all be Scorpios. I have no statistics on how these marriages work out. I have a feeling that some do and others don't.

Ottilia *(German) "Heroine"*

There is some disagreement on whether this means just a heroine, or a battle heroine, and whether or not it is the feminine form of Otto. I'm inclined to give it to the warlike signs, Aries and Scorpio. Odile is the preferred version in some parts, and it is easier to spell.

Queenie *(English) "Queen"*

The leaders of the Zodiac include Leo, Aries, and Scorpio. This is also a name frequently given to dogs.

SCORPIO

Rebecca *(Hebrew) "Ensnarer"*

And didn't I have a time with that! Everyone agrees the word comes from some kind of binding, but what does that mean? Various onomasts suggested "a knotted cord" or "a yoke," while one authority came right out and suggested "noose." The optimistic onomasts suggested it meant "one bound in the service of the Lord." In the end, though, the majority made it out to mean that Rebecca was another Delilah or Lorelei type. Various forms of the name include Reba, Riva, and Becky. The most famous Beckys in literature, Becky Thatcher and Becky Sharp, seem to have been written by men who definitely had the "yoke" and "ensnarer" in mind.

Ruth *(Hebrew) "Beautiful friend"*

Libra, Scorpio, and Pisces are the best-looking signs in the Zodiac, and though Libra and Pisces are more friendly on a person-to-person basis, Scorpio is the type to make a small number of friends and remain fiercely loyal to them (provided the friends don't slip up). Ruthi and Ruthie are pet forms.

Tempest *(English) "Tempest"*

This is for someone who is stormy, tempestuous. Tempestuous is a very flattering way of saying ill-tempered, but I guess we're not supposed to notice. Aries and Scorpio would go well with the name.

Theresa *(Greek, Italian, Spanish, or something) "Harvester"*

Libra and Scorpio are the signs of harvest time. In addition, Theresa seems to have become identified with hot-tempered Spanish beauties. (I understand there are Spanish beauties who are perfectly agreeable people, but I'm not one to go around stomping on people's stereotypes.) There are plenty of variants, including Teresa, Tess, Tracy, Resa, Riza, and Therese.

Valerie *(Latin) "Strong"*

The physically strong signs of the Zodiac are Aries, Taurus, Leo, Scorpio, and Sagittarius. Variants include Valya and Valeriana. I am inclined, myself, to see "valor" in the name, as well, but the onomasts do not support me there.

Vera *(Latin) "Truth" (Russian) "Faith"*

Scorpio and Sagittarius are deeply concerned with both, though Scorpio is a bit fiercer about it. Variants include Verushka, Verenne, and Viriane. Some people include Veronica and some don't.

Zuleika *(Arabic) "Brilliant, beautiful"*

Beautiful signs are Libra, Scorpio, and Pisces. Scorpio would probably go farthest with an exotic name that people will always be asking her how to pronounce. A variant is Zeleeka, which may give you a hint.

SCORPIO
BOYS' NAMES

Akim *(Hebrew) "God will establish"*

This is a short form, through Russian, of Jehoiakim, and it is no problem to understand why you don't see *that* one much these days. Aries, Leo, and Scorpio have no trouble believing they have been established by a higher power. The problem is convincing them that there is anything higher than they are.

Arnold *(German) "Eagle"*

This is, as mentioned, one of the symbols of the positive side of Scorpio. Arn and Arnie are pet forms. Variants are Arnaud, Arnott, and Arndt.

Baldwin *(German) "Bold friend"*

Scorpio is bold, and makes a fast friend. Baudouin is sometimes used as a variant. I can't see any pet forms except the obvious one.

Blake *(Anglo-Saxon) "Dark"*

Just to confuse things, though, some onomasts feel this means "fair, light." I think the basic problem is that they don't know whether this comes from blanc (white) or black (guess). You may take your pick. Scorpio is likely to be dark-complected, and, anyway, these short, sharp names are very in, just now, for the Scorpios who inhabit the soap operas.

Brian *(Norse) "Strong"*

Physically strong signs are Aries, Taurus, Leo, Scorpio, and Sagittarius. Variants are Bryan and Bryant. There have been attempts at feminine forms with Brianne and Brienne, but this seems like an awful lot of effort to me.

Casey *(Celtic) "Brave"*

Signs known for their courage include Scorpio, Aries, Leo, and Sagittarius. This is sometimes used as a short form for Casimir, and is commonly applied to boys or girls whose initials are K.C., or who come from Kansas City.

Cedric *(Celtic) "Leader"*

This is another title for those aristocrats, Leo, Aries, and Scorpio. Cedric has had a bad rap much of this century as a name for an ultrarefined (read "wimpy") Englishman. We seem to be growing out of this, but I would avoid the pet form, Ceddie, for a few more decades if I were you.

Dustin *(German) "Valiant fighter"*

This is for the warlike signs, Aries and Scorpio. The nickname is Dusty, which has a kind of a cowboy ring to it. They tell me there is a feminine form, Dustine.

Dirk *(German) "Dirk"*

Actually, this is a form of Derek, Dietrich, and Theodoric. Nonetheless, it is really a name for a soap opera Scorpio, not only because it is brief and to the point, but also because it signifies a kind of knife, generally seen in books and in movies, stuck between the teeth of pirates as they swarm aboard a ship.

Duncan *(Gaelic) "Dark warrior"*

Aries and Scorpio, the warlike signs, should get this. Dunc is the nickname.

SCORPIO

Elnathan *(Hebrew) "God-given"*

See John, under Aries boys, for notes on this and other "gift" names. Elnathan is, of course, Nathaniel turned around. It has never been a common name, but I fell in love with the name "Elnathan Stone" in the Uncle Abner detective stories by Melville Davisson Post. As far as I can recall, though Elnathan Stone appeared in several stories, he hardly ever did anything. But he *sounded* so solid and dignified.

Erwin *(Anglo-Saxon) "Sea-friend"*

Scorpio is a fast friend, and also one of the water signs. Irwin is a variant. There is some argument among onomasts about this meaning, and some hold that Irvin, Ervin, and Irving are entirely separate names.

Gerald *(German) "Mighty spearman"*

This is another one of those German warrior names that doesn't sound so impressive today. But these things change. We never know when a hero named Gerald may rise from nowhere to change our perceptions. It is not at all the fault of Gerald R. Ford, former President of the United States, though he didn't help all that much, either. Jerry is the nickname. Geraldo, Giraldo, Gerard, and Gerhard are variants. Geraldine, of course, is the feminine form.

Harlan *(German) "Land of warriors"*

Aries or Scorpio would make it in a place like that.

Heathcliff *(English) "From the cliff of the wasteland"*

Scorpio would feel right at home in such a desolate place. The most famous of the Heathcliffs was a Scorpio type whose intense drive for whatever it is haunts one of the great Gothic novels, *Wuthering Heights.*

Herman *(German) "Warrior"*

Aries and Scorpio are the warriors of the Zodiac. Ermano is a variant, which brings it dangerously close to the Spanish word for brother. This is, no doubt, a coincidence.

SCORPIO

Jacob *(Hebrew) "Supplanter"*

A supplanter is one who gets in and replaces you, snatches your job, takes over what is yours. Aries, Capricorn, and Scorpio are prone to this. The name Jacob has gone through an amazing variety of names, including Iago, Santiago (literally "Saint Iago"), Jacopo, Jacques, Jake, James, Jock, Jocko, Jack, Jakob, Yakov, Shamus, and Seamus. It is not, apparently, related to the slang word "shamus" meaning a private eye, but comes from another Hebrew origin entirely.

Kirk *(German) "Church"*

In fact, this is still used as a word in Scotland. Taurus and Scorpio are, each in his own way, devout.

Marmaduke *(Celtic) "A sea leader"*

The water signs are Scorpio, Cancer, and Pisces. Scorpio is the leader in this group.

Martin *(Latin) "Warlike"*

Closely related to Mark, this is another name for warlike Aries and Scorpio. Marty and Martyn are variants.

Merle *(Latin)*

The onomasts haven't come to a consensus yet on this, though they agree it signifies something dark, probably a dark bird, and perhaps a falcon, particularly the falcon known as a merlin. Scorpio has all the qualities necessary to emulate this fierce carnivore. Variants include Merlin, of course, with Marlin and Marlon.

Morrell *(Latin) "Dark, swarthy"*

Taurus and Scorpio are likely to have dark complexions. Some people accent this on the first syllable and some prefer the second.

SCORPIO

Nigel *(Celtic)* *"Champion"*

If you use the meaning of someone who is the best, the winner, it should go to Aries, Leo, or Scorpio. But if you prefer the old meaning of someone who fights for a cause, then Scorpio and Aquarius might be a better bet.

Norman *(English)* *"Norman"*

The Normans come from Normandy, but before they got there and became Normans, they were Norsemen, Vikings in search of plunder. (By the way, why isn't the plural of Norman Normen?) Aries and Scorpio are the Viking-like characters. Norm is the nickname form. The feminine form is *not* Norma, say the experts, and they should know. There is some tendency to use Normandy or Normandie for girls.

Roger *(German)* *"Famous spearman"*

Aries and Scorpio are the warriors, but Leo can fight too, particularly if there is fame involved. Rog (generally pronounced Rodge, but sometimes the way it's spelled) is the nickname. Ruggiero and Hrothgar are acceptable variants, if you feel like it. I don't like to bring the matter up, but not so long ago "roger" was a slang verb with a meaning apparently derived from the custom, centuries ago, of naming bulls Roger. The word has given way to older and more pungent verbs these days, but it does still turn up now and again.

Roman *(Latin)* *"Roman"*

The Romans have a reputation for culture. All the culture the Romans ever had they imported from Greece. What they were really good at was conquest and bureaucracy. For conquest, you have Leo, Aries, and Scorpio. For bureaucracy, try Virgo and Capricorn. Romain is sometimes used as a variant, but you run the risk of getting it mixed up with the lettuce.

Titus *(Greek)* *"Of the Titans"*

Aries, Leo, and Scorpio are larger than life. Tito is a variant.

Ulysses *(Greek)* *"Angry"*

If you stick to the meaning, you may give it to Scorpio, an ill-tempered sign.

SCORPIO

If you prefer to think of Ulysses as the great hero of mythology, give the name to Aries, Leo, or Scorpio. Or you might recall Ulysses as a redheaded hero who got his reputation because he loved to scheme and bamboozle. In that case, Sagittarius might suit the name. Or you may know Ulysses as the name of a dirty book. I can't help you with that—you are beyond help.

Victor *(Latin) "Winner"*

The one that got the victory, see? This should go to Scorpio, Aries, or Leo.

Walter *(German) "Powerful warrior"*

Aries and Scorpio are the warriors of the Zodiac. Several onomasts insist that this means "Rule folk," in which case the rulers, Aries, Leo, and Scorpio get it. Wat, Walt, and Wally are pet forms. Gauthier is a variant.

SAGITTARIUS

the Archer

November 22 to December 21

If Sagittarius has a name, it's probably Indiana Jones. Sagittarians go for the gusto in life; they are the swashbucklers, the gamblers, the free spirits. They love freedom and the wide open spaces. They seek adventure.

Even when they don't seek it, they're likely to get it. Though tolerant, Sagittarians are outspoken. They are great seekers after truth, and when they don't find any, they're likely to say something about it. Sagittarians get carried away in causes, and go their length. They can't help this. They have only one speed—full—and their brakes don't always work.

Unconventional, inventive, lively, sometimes irresponsible, they are nonetheless subject to occasional fits of depression—generally lucid periods in which they realize all this rushing around isn't getting them anywhere. If they can harness their energy, they are capable of great things. Sagittarians have great memory capacity, though it tends to operate only within areas that interest them. The old joke about the scientist who ordered acetylsalicylic acid at the drugstore because he couldn't remember the word aspirin probably involved a Sagittarius.

Semi-famous Sagittarians include Frances Hodgson Burnett, Ellis Parker Butler, Jack Cole, Percy Crosby, Emily Dickinson, E. R. Eddison, Shirley Jackson, Munro Leaf, H. H. Munro, Arch Oboler, Charles Schulz, Elzie Segar, E. H. Shepard, Donald Ogden Stewart, Rex Stout, Albert Payson Terhune, James Thurber, and John R. Tunis.

SAGITTARIUS
GIRLS' NAMES

Angela *(Greek) "Heavenly messenger"*

Gemini and Sagittarius are the folks that make good messengers; they like being the bearers of tidings, good or bad. The masculine forms of this are Angel and Angelo. Variant forms for women include Ange, Angel, Angie, Angelique, Angelian, and Angelica.

Ashley *(Anglo-Saxon) "Ash tree meadow"*

Ash is a popular wood, used in this country mainly for sporting equipment. Sagittarius likes living trees, but will be able to make do with ash in the form of skis, too. It is a name for boys or girls, but for some reason is given mainly to girls these days. Variant forms from the inventive include Ashleigh and Ashlea.

Audrey *(Anglo-Saxon) "Noble strength"*

The people most likely to be physically strong are born under Taurus, Aries, Leo, Scorpio, and Sagittarius. There are some exotic variants of this: Audra, Audie, Audrina, Etheldreda, and Aethelthryth.

Blaze *(English) "Blaze"*

I suppose a case could be made for this being a feminine form of Blaise, but why bother? Everyone uses it for just what it sounds like. It should probably go to one of the fire signs, Sagittarius, Aries, or Leo, and it has a snappy sound that would suit it for Sagittarius.

Blythe *(Anglo-Saxon) "Glad, joyous"*

Sagittarius can be one of the most cheerful of the signs of the Zodiac, though she can't keep it up all the time. This is sometimes pronounced with a hard th, as in "the," and sometimes with a soft th, as in "think."

SAGITTARIUS

Brandy *(English)* *"Brandy"*

This is a potent brew, with a jaunty sort of name. It sounds just right for Sagittarius. Some experts say this is the feminine form of Brandon.

Clara *(Latin)* *"Clear"*

Taurus, Sagittarius, and Pisces are the kinds of people to see things clearly. It's what they're likely to do about what they see that differs. Clare, Claire, Claretta, and Clarice are variants. Some people add Clarissa, and some feel it is a separate name. Clare and Clair are both used for boys as well as girls.

Diane *(Latin)* *"Goddess of the moon"*

Actually, some people have traced this name back even further, and have found evidence that shows its literal meaning is "Belonging to the female divinity." That's going back a little too far for most of us. Diana was the Roman name for the Greek goddess Artemis, moon goddess and huntress. For the moon, you can give this name to Cancer, but to most people it will always be "Diana, the Huntress of the Woods," which is more in Sagittarius's line. Dee is a pet form, as is Di, if you didn't already know that. Deanna, Deanne, and Dyan are variants.

Elizabeth *(Hebrew)* *"Oath of God"*

I have seen no reports on what is the name with the largest number of variants. Katherine, Margaret, and Helen are all right there in the top ten, but Elizabeth is famous for its versatility. Anything this widespread must be the sort of thing for Sagittarius or Gemini, but there are so many forms there's probably one for everybody. Some of them are Elsa, Elspeth, Eliza, Elissa, Elsie, Lisa, Liza, Ilsa, Lizzie, Ellie, Libby, Beth, Betty, Bette, Bettina, Betsy, Bess, Bessie, Isabel, Liese, Tetty, and Tibby. Some people include Bethany, though I have my doubts, and others add both Lily and Lili. There's Lillibet and Bitzy and Lila and...This is how onomasts get to be the way they are.

Elvira *(Spanish)* *"White, fair"*

Many onomasts try to get elves into the meaning somewhere, making it "elfin." Sagittarius can be fair to look at, in her own way, and she is occasionally elfin, as well. This would do for Gemini or Aquarius, too. Elva and Elvina are variants.

Evangeline *(Greek) "Bringer of good news"*

Gemini and Sagittarius get this since it is another "messenger" name. People familiar with the poem "Evangeline" will continue to think of her as a heroine of the wilderness, but, alas, this group gets smaller every year. Eva is used as a pet form.

Eve *(Hebrew) "Life"*

Gemini, Aquarius, Sagittarius, Aries, Scorpio, and Leo are the lively signs of the Zodiac. Or you may prefer to remember that Eve was the first woman, and give the name to one of the feminine signs of the Zodiac, which are Pisces, Capricorn, Scorpio, Virgo, Cancer, and Taurus. There are plenty of variants to go around: Evie, Eva, Ava, Ewe, Evette, and Evita are some of them. Evelyn, a name for men and women, with its pet forms, Lina, Lena, Lynn, and Ev, is a side issue. Though most onomasts agree this is a form of Eve, some add a note to the effect that it may be instead derived from the name Evelina, which may come from aveline, a word for the hazelnut. I feel this is carrying research a little too far.

Felicia *(Latin) "Happy"*

Pisces, Sagittarius, Aquarius, and Leo are some of the more cheerful signs of the Zodiac. Variants are Felicity, Felice, Feliz, and Felicidad. The masculine form, of course, is Felix.

Frances *(Latin) "Free"*

This is for Sagittarius, Aquarius, and Gemini, those signs that seem to have a desire for freedom that amounts to restlessness. Some onomasts prefer to say this means "from France," but there's doubtless a reasonable explanation. The masculine form is Francis. Francine and Fanchetta are a couple of feminine variants. Nicknames for women include Fran, Frank, Frankie, and Fanny. The slang meaning of fanny in this country has caused it to slip a bit in popularity. If you go abroad, fanny almost always means something anatomical, but it doesn't always refer to the same part of the body. So watch out.

SAGITTARIUS

Gale *(Anglo-Saxon) "Lively"*

The lively signs are, as noted under Eve, Gemini, Aquarius, Sagittarius, Aries, Scorpio, and Leo. Any of them would also get along with the other, more common, meaning of gale: a high force wind. Gayle, Gayleen, Gayle, and Gail are variants.

Ginger *(Latin) "Ginger"*

This is a spice, regarded as exotic and exciting. It is the sort of thing for Scorpio, Sagittarius, Gemini, and any redhead. I am not certain how this is related to the adverb "gingerly."

Heather *(Anglo-Saxon) "Heather"*

Romantic types view heather as an exciting plant, existing on windblown plains where lovers rush into each other's arms. This is the kind of thing Sagittarius would go for. Less romantic types cannot see the glory of an undeveloped field full of weeds. I do not know what to do about these people, but couldn't we all get together and think of something?

Helen *(Greek) "Light"*

This should probably go to a fire sign: Aries, Leo, or Sagittarius, particularly with reference to the original Helen, Helen of Troy, who certainly set the world on fire, or at least her little corner of it. But, as with Katherine, Elizabeth, and several others, there are enough variants around that you can probably find one for use with any sign. These include Ellen, Elaine, Aileen, Eileen, Elena, Eleanor, Elanor, Lena, Lana, Lenore, Nora, Nell, Nelly, Nellie, Alianor, Ilene, Elinor, Lanie, and probably dozens of others. Some savant, years ago, tried to introduce the word "helen" as a unit of measurement for beauty. This year's blonde, for example, would be measured at, say, fifty kilohelens, while the rest of us would be measured in millihelens. It doesn't seem to have caught on, because what would you use for a yardstick?

Hyacinth *(Greek) "Hyacinth"*

A hyacinth is a purple flower, and purple is one of Sagittarius's colors. There is a jewel known as a jacinth, which is the same color, and Jacinth has also been used as a girl's name.

SAGITTARIUS

Jean *(Hebrew)* *"God's gracious gift"*

See John, under Aries boys, and Jane, under Virgo girls, for details. Jeanne is a variant, particularly in France, where Jean is the masculine form of the name. It has, however, led to the creation of JeAnne, a two-syllable name which makes me queasy. Still, there was a perfectly fine medieval French name spelled Jehanne, so maybe it's just me.

Joy *(English)* *"Joy"*

Leo, Sagittarius, Gemini, Aquaqrius, and Pisces are inclined to be joyful, though Sagittarius and Pisces are considered the jovial signs. Joia is a variant.

Kay *(Greek)* *"Rejoice"*

Oh, the onomasts have had a field day. Some say this is a form of Gay, and some say it's a form of Katherine. A few insist it's a pet name for just any-one whose name begins with K. But the majority lean toward "rejoice," and it should go to one of the cheerful signs listed under Joy. Kai is a variant, usually used only as a reference to Sir Kai, one of King Arthur's grouchier knights.

Millicent *(German)* *"Strength"*

Aries, Taurus, Leo, Scorpio, and Sagittarius are most likely to be physically strong. There are lots of ways to spell this: Melicent, Melisande, Melisant, and so forth. Millie and Missy are the usual nickname forms.

Minnehaha *(American Indian)* *"Laughing water"*

The joke is on me, it seems. I always assumed Longfellow just made this name up for his poem about Hiawatha, and some wag later made the joke that it meant "laughing water" because of the "ha ha" in it. But I am wrong; it is the name of Hiawatha's wife, and it really does mean "laughing water." I apologize to any Minnehahas I may have offended. But, with so many smart alecks in the world, perhaps Minnehahas are used to this sort of problem. There can't be many of them these days, not since Longfellow's reputation as the be-all and end-all of American poetry started to slip. In her day,though, Minnehaha was regarded as a heroine of the wilderness, the sort of thing Sagittarius would like (and Sagittarius could probably put up with the jokes, too). Minnehaha's death scene impressed so many

Victorians that plenty of little girls were named Minnehaha in those days. I ran across one young lady who registered for college, signing her name "Minnie-ha ha!!" Her father was President of the Board of Trustees at the time, so they let her enroll anyhow.

Pixy *(English) "Pixy"*

This is also spelled Pixie, particularly when used as a name instead of a noun. This is a perky little name for Gemini, Aquarius, or Sagittarius. What with computers and their pixels entering common speech, this name might become more widespread. Please do not name your twins Pixie and Dixie. It's been done.

Sylvia *(Latin) "Forest"*

Outdoorsy Sagittarius will enjoy this, if she can get around that song by Shakespeare that has been imposed on singing classes for years, and begins "Who is Sylvia? What is she?" It goes on to say that she is wondrous fair, but it's that first line that does the damage. Sylvie, Silvia, and Sylvette are variants. Sylvester is the most common masculine form.

Valentina *(Latin) "Strong, brave"*

Aries, Leo, Scorpio, Sagittarius, and Taurus tend to be strong, and they're generally brave as well. The first woman in space was named Valentina, but that was probably before your time. Variants are Valencia, Valensia, Valeda, Valentine, and Tina. Valentine is also sometimes given to men.

Veronica *(Latin) "True image"*

Sagittarius and Capricorn are least likely to try to present the world with a false front, Sagittarius because it inclines toward an open, guileless attitude, and Capricorn because of its "I yam what I yam" philosophy. People argue about which names are or aren't variants., Veronique seems pretty definite, but others add Vera, Vonni, Berenice, and Bernice.

Yvonne *(French) "Archer"*

This is obviously Sagittarius's sort of thing. Some onomasts make this a form of John, by way of Ivan or Evan or Yves. The pronunciation is also up for grabs, some people saying Ee-von, and some saying Ya-von. You may take your pick. Iva, Yva, and Yvette are sometimes considered variants.

SAGITTARIUS
BOYS' NAMES

Angus *(Celtic)* *"Exceptionally strong"*

Aries, Taurus, Leo, Scorpio, and Sagittarius are the signs that produce physically strong people. You used to have to be Scottish to get away with this name; I expect you still do.

Asher *(Hebrew)* *"Happy, fortunate"*

Jupiter rules Sagittarius and Pisces. What has this got to do with anything? Well, Jupiter was also known as Jove, and people born under his sign were expected to be jovial. No, I did not just make that up; all the planets are supposed to affect you that way, at least, all the planets known to the ancients. People controlled by Mercury are mercurial, people born under Mars are martial, people born under Saturn are saturnine. Would this make people born under Venus venal or venereal, do you suppose? No one has bothered to tell me whether persons born under Cancer, the lunar sign, are thus lunatics. Maybe they just moon around a lot.

Beren

This is the third and final Tolkien name stolen for this book. This time I know it was one of his own creations, but I like the sound of it, especially if I'm pronouncing it right by rhyming it with Karen or baron. Tolkien seems to have given no hint to its meaning, but Beren was one of the great heroes of his tales, an adventurer with drive and purpose. I'd assign it to Sagittarius or Scorpio. You could always use Barry as a nickname.

Bevis *(German)* *"Bow"*

That's bow as in what an archer carries, which should make its placement obvious. Not all onomasts are happy with "bow"; some derive it from a

SAGITTARIUS

French name, Beauvais, meaning a place with a nice view. If it makes them happy, I will not bicker.

Brandon *(Anglo-Saxon)* *"Beacon hill"*

Something is amiss, and someone has lit the signal flares on top of a hill to tell everyone for miles around that the game is afoot. The adventure and excitement of the sign obviously belong to Sagittarius. Sagittarius is also one of the fire signs. Some people use Brand as a nickname form.

Bruce *(French)* *"From the brushwood thicket"*

This is for outdoorsy Sagittarius. In addition, most Bruces are named after Robert Bruce, the Scottish king.

Bud *(Anglo-Saxon)* *"Messenger"*

I suppose this symbolizes the fact that the buds on the trees bring news that spring is coming. Gemini and Sagittarius are the best choices for messengers; they love to get there first with the latest. Bud is also short for buddy; yelling "Hey, bud!" at someone you don't know is derived from "Hey, buddy!" which gained wide acceptance during and after World War I, when "buddy" was used that way between servicemen. (The message communicated was "Hey, I don't know you, but we're both in uniform, so we might as well do each other favors.") This in turn goes back to the mid-nineteenth century, when it was taken from the baby talk form of "brother." It's amazing how far you can go, just looking up one three-letter word. Bud is sometimes used as a nickname for Bernard.

Buster *(English)* *"Buster"*

Well, no one quite knows why this become a name. In the nineteenth century, going into town on a spree was known as "going on a buster." If you have ever witnessed a traditional drinking party, particularly on a college campus, the appropriateness of this term will be obvious to you. Some say the name comes from Buster Keaton, who says he got his name from Harry Houdini, who watched him fall down a flight of stairs once. But the comic strip Buster Brown was running in those days, too, and the name might come from there. Only one onomast I checked even listed the name, and defined it as "A jovial boy." That's reasonable.

SAGITTARIUS

Charles (French) "Manly, strong"

The masculine signs of the Zodiac are Aries, Gemini, Leo, Libra, Sagittarius, and Aquarius. The ones known for strength are Aries, Taurus, Leo, Scorpio, and Sagittarius. You may take your pick. The name comes from a word for "man" in several languages. Kerl is still used in German, and ceorl, or churl, is still bopping around in historical novels in English. There are plenty of variant forms of the name: Karl, Carl, Carlos, Karel, Charlie, Charley, Chuck, Caryl, Cary, Carroll, and so on. There are also plenty of female forms, for some reason, including Charlotte, Carlotta, Cheryl, Charlene, Sharla, and Carol.

Cornelius (Latin) "Horn"

Aries, Gemini, Leo, and Sagittarius are the noisier signs of the Zodiac. A variant is Corneille. The feminine form is Cornelia. You will notice that the onomasts insist that the masculine form means horn, while the feminine form means horn-colored, or yellow. I don't know what this means, unless it's some odd form of chivalry.

Dennis (French) "Dionysius"

That's Bacchus, to some of you, the classical god of wine. He is often depicted as a fat old souse, but that version is not, properly speaking, Bacchus. It is Silenus. Dionysius was one of the younger gods, a bouncy, irrepressible soul who investigated the grape and introduced wine to the gods of Mt. Olympus with results that he, at least, giggled about for centuries afterward. He also invented the dolphin. The name gained much popularity from St. Denis, the patron saint of Paris, whose tomb was built on a hill he walked to after he was beheaded. Denys is a variant. Feminine forms are Denice and Denise.

Dwight (German) "White, fair"

To many people this is the name for a knight errant, a knight in shining armor, with clear eyes and a dimpled chin. He slays the dragon and gets the girl. A Sagittarius type, I think. Sagittarians love to go out and kill dragons (though they are sometimes nonplussed to find themselves stuck with the princess).

Eric *(German) "Ever powerful"*

This sounds like a name for the strong men of the Zodiac again: Aries, Taurus, Leo, Scorpio, Sagittarius. Rick and Ricky are used as nickname forms. Erica is the feminine form, but many people prefer Erin, which is another name altogether.

Ferdinand *(German) "Bold travel"*

Sagittarius and Aquarius are the lovers of travel; Gemini likes a change of scene from time to time as well. If you must name your Taurus after Ferdinand the Bull, I suppose you can go ahead. Variant forms include Fernando and Hernando.

Forrest *(Latin) "Woodland"*

Surprised? This is a name for the outdoorsy Sagittarius. A lot of people use Woody as the nickname form of this. A lot of people put salt on their watermelon, too. Forry is another nickname.

Franklin *(German) "Free man"*

Freedom is much, sometimes all, to Aquarius and Sagittarius. This is obviously related to Francis, and the nickname Frank serves for both.

Gaylord *(French) "Bold, cheerful nobleman"*

That's as clear a description of many of the great swashbucklers of history as you could possibly want. It belongs to Sagittarius or Leo.

Igor *(Scandinavian) "Hero"*

Sagittarius, Aquarius, and Scorpio are the types to go out and make heroes of themselves. The movies have made this into a joke name, though, making him the sometimes comic, sometimes sinister sidekick of the mad scientist. A variant, Ygor, has the same problem.

Joseph *(Hebrew) "God will add"*

This speaks of an optimism that clearly belongs to Leo and Sagittarius.

There are lots of variants: Josef, José, Giuseppe, Joe, Joey, Joie, Yusuf, Pepe, Pepito, and Beppo. Some onomasts say the Puritan name Increase was a literal translation. I can see that, I guess.

Leonard *(German)* *"Brave as a lion"*

You thought I'd put this under Leo, didn't you? But it would be silly to say a lion is brave as a lion, wouldn't it? Aries, Scorpio, and Sagittarius are brave. Variants of Leonard are Len, Lenny, and Leonardo.

Lucius *(Latin)* *"Light" or "Bringer of light"*

It should probably go to one of the fire signs, Aries, Leo, or Sagittarius. The bringer of light was Prometheus, a rapscallion with Sagittarian tendencies. The gods had decided to let mankind freeze to death, thus relieving the earth of its burden, but Prometheus sneaked down to them with fire. It's the kind of thing Sagittarius or Aquarius would do. Luc and Luke are nicknames; other variants are Lucio, Lucian, Lucas, and Luciano.

Peregrine *(Latin)* *"Traveler"*

Another word for travels is peregrinations. Try that one on your friends and watch their mouths drop open. You may take this as a gloomy word for a homeless wanderer and give it to Scorpio or Capricorn. Or you may think of it simply as someone who likes to get around, and give it to Gemini, Sagittarius, and Aquarius. Perry is used as a short form, though some onomasts make it a separate name.

Pippin

This is the name, or, rather, the nickname, of one of Tolkien's Hobbits. (His real name is Peregrine.) But it has a long history among real names, being considered either a nickname for Phillip or a form of Pepin, the name of a long line of French kings who lived much too long ago. It is also a variety of apple. The jaunty sound of it would serve a Sagittarius well, as would the even shorter form, Pip.

Rhett *(Welsh)* *"Ardent, enthusiastic"*

This is Sagittarius all over, and also fits Gemini. Naturally, anyone named Rhett these days is named for Rhett Butler, but a Sagittarius would think that's just fine. Another form of the name is Reece.

Russell *(Latin)* *"Redhead"*

Redheads are supposed to be hot, spicy, and adventurous. Leo, Aries, and Sagittarius like the idea. Russ and Rusty are pet forms.

Salvador *(Spanish)* *"Savior"*

If you take this as a religious reference, it had best go to one of the devout signs, Taurus or Scorpio. But if you want it for someone who's into going around saving people, try Sagittarius.

Sylvester *(Latin)* *"Forest"*

This is another name for outdoorsy Sagittarius. Mind you, he will spend his life having people sneak up behind him to yell "I tawt I taw a puddy tat!" But if it wasn't that, it would be something else.

Theodore *(Greek)* *"God's gift"*

See John, under Aries boys, for the gift names. A lot of Theodores are named after Theodore Roosevelt, an eternal extrovert, cowboy, soldier, crusading politician, leather-lunged orator, and physical fitness nut. This is a fine example for Sagittarius. (Teddy Roosevelt was a Scorpio, by the way, but I'm sure a deeper study of his chart would explain all this.) Variants include Fyodor, Teodoro, Tudor, and Theo. The onomasts insist Theodoric is a separate name. Ted and Teddy are pet forms.

Todd *(English)* *"Fox"*

The sly old fox is a frequent character in folk tales, but doesn't seem to appear in very many names. He is, however, a Sagittarian clean clear through. In Disney's movie *The Fox and the Hound* they named the fox Todd, and the hound Copper, presumably because to catch something is to cop it. Another example of onomastics in action.

Virgil *(Latin)* *"Strong, flourishing"*

Aries, Leo, Taurus, and Sagittarius are the most robust of the twelve signs. Vergil is a variant spelling.

SAGITTARIUS

Winston *(Anglo-Saxon)* *"Friendly farm"*

Aries, Taurus, Leo, Libra, Sagittarius, and Aquarius are the most affable of folks. Some Sagittarians might find farm life tame, while others would consider it a major challenge. Winnie, Win, and Wynn are pet forms. Winton is a variant if you don't want people asking him whether he tastes good like a cigarette should.

CAPRICORN
the Sea Goat
December 22 to January 21

No one really knows what a sea goat is. Don't worry about it.

The sign is ruled by the planet Saturn, which makes people saturnine: gloomy, dour, aloof. Capricorn is cool, perhaps a bit calculating; all the experts claim Capricorns are the ones most likely to marry for money.

Capricorn is orderly and hard-working, like Virgo, but adds intolerance to it. Though respectful of superiors, elders, and traditional ways, Capricorn has very little use for underlings. "Don't ask questions; do what I tell you" is Capricorn's way of handling subordinates. Advice, no matter how nicely worded, will not be accepted. Popeye's motto, "I yam what I yam," is Capricorn's motto.

Predictably, Capricorn is conservative and discreet. Though passionate, Capricorns exercise caution around the opposite sex. They often *seem* to be flirting; actually, they feel uncomfortable around the opposite sex and are trying to assert control by throwing the other person off balance.

Capricorns are long-lived, generally coming into their own around middle age. They tend to be popular and have many friends. (They are probably so pessimistic that everyone thinks they're joking.) Though exceedingly ambitious and capable of taking on massive amounts of work, they are born under what is considered the unluckiest sign of the Zodiac.

Semi-famous Capricorns include Charles Addams, Peter Arno, Howard Chandler Christy, Harold Gray, John R. Held Jr., Robert E. Howard, Stephen Leacock, Fritz Leiber Jr., Hugh Lofting, A. A. Milne (and Eeyore), Fitz-James O'Brien, Frederick Burr Opper, Robert W. Service, Clark Ashton Smith, Otto Soglow, and Chic Young.

CAPRICORN
GIRLS' NAMES

Aida *(Italian)* *"Prosperous"*

This is an exotic form of Ada for the prosperous signs of the Zodiac: Taurus, Capricorn, and Leo.

Arabella *(Latin)* *"Beautiful altar"*

Pisces, Capricorn, and Cancer are the folks most likely to appreciate the art and the traditions behind an artistic altar. Arbel, Arabel, and Orabelle are variants.

Aurelia *(Latin)* *"Gold"*

As a color, this is Leo's sort of thing, but regarded as money, it also belongs to Taurus and Capricorn. Aurel, Orelia, Orela, Ora, Aurora, and Aura Lee are variants.

Beryl *(Hebrew)* *"Beryl"*

This is a precious gem that is supposed to have the power to make the wearer invincible in war or in a lawsuit. Although a talisman like this would obviously be useful to just about anyone, why not give it to Capricorn and see if it can counteract her traditional bad luck? It can be pronounced to rhyme with Merle or Cheryl. As Burl, it is sometimes given to boys, though some people feel this is a separate name.

Blanche *(French)* *"White"*

This can apply to anyone, but if it makes you think of snow, Capricorn, Aquarius, and Pisces are your best bets. There are several variants forms and spellings, including Blanca, Bianca, Branca, Bellanca, and Blinni.

Carol *(Latin)* *"Strong, manly"*

This is a form of Charles, for which, see Cheryl, under Leo girls. Some do derive it from a joyous song, as in Christmas carols, and that is certainly what it means to a lot of people who hear it. There are lots of variants, including Carole, Carleen, Carla, Carly, Caroline, Carolina, Charo, Carrie, Cary, Karla, Carlotta, Lotta, Lola, Lolita, Lotte, Charlotte, Charleen, Sharla, Sherlyn, Sherrilyn, Sherry, and so on.

Claudia *(Latin) "Lame*

This can be applied to the more hesitant folk in the Zodiac, Cancer, Gemini, Pisces, and Libra. Or it may be considered a symbol of the bad luck of Capricorn. Claudette and Claudine are feminine forms; some people also include Gladys. Claude is the masculine form.

Colleen *(Gaelic) "Girl"*

This is a name for a youthful-looking sign, like Gemini, Virgo, or Capricorn. The name Colin is closely related.

Consuelo *(Spanish) "Consolation"*

Capricorn, Cancer, Virgo, and Scorpio always need to be consoled for something. The original form was Consuelo, another title of the Virgin Mary, but people started spelling it with an A on the end, Consuela, because it looked more like a girl's name that way. Connie is the nickname form.

Deirdre *(Gaelic) "Sorrows"*

This is one of the most commonly known name meanings. Everybody seems to know it: "Deirdre of the Sorrows." Deirdre and sorrows go together like Chicago and machine guns.

But the onomasts hate it when everybody already knows something, so they have been digging deeper, to come up with a sparkling array of meanings, from "one whose rage causes fear" to "complete wanderer." I'm sticking to sorrows, though, and awarding this to Cancer and Capricorn. Fifty million Frenchmen can't be wrong.

One reason for Deirdre's sorrows may be that nobody knows how to spell the name. This is one name where all the variants started out as misspellings, like Deidra, Deedra, Deadra, and so on. Dee and Deedee are the common nickname forms.

CAPRICORN

Dinah *(Hebrew) "Vindicated"*

Scorpio and Capricorn are always feeling wronged, and work to vindicate themselves before the world, even when the world doesn't especially care. Dominique is supposed to be the French form of the name. If so, then Dominick is a related name for boys.

Enid *(Welsh) "Purity"*

Enid was known in traditional tales as a woman of spotless and indomitable virtue. Capricorn is inclined to set up such rigid standards, for herself and for others as well.

Hazel *(English) "Hazel"*

This refers to a shrub and also to a color, a shade of light brown. Both Leo and Capricorn have light brown among their traditional colors. Witch hazel is a common home remedy which any girl named Hazel will have to cope with. There is also Ted Key's immortal cartoon (and TV) character, but she makes a pretty fair role model.

Heidi *(German) "Prosperous"*

This is another form of Ada, for the prosperous signs, Taurus, Capricorn, and Leo. In addition, it is the name of one of those immortal children in literature, a cheerful soul whose name might help counteract Capricorn's gloom.

Holly *(English) "Holly"*

This is a traditional plant of the Christmas season, mostly associated with Sagittarius, but traditional for Capricorn as well. Holly is supposed to bring luck, too, and heaven knows Capricorn could use some.

Iva *(Hebrew) "God's gracious gift"*

See John, under Aries boys, and Jane, under Virgo girls, for notes on "gift" names. Yvonne and Yvette are sometimes used as variant forms, and some people use Ivy as a nickname.

CAPRICORN

Jacqueline *(Hebrew) "Supplanter"*

This comes out of Jacob by way of Jacques and is a very popular girl's name, particularly trendy during the Kennedy administration. Supplanters are, as noted under Jacob, Scorpio, Aries, and Capricorn. Variant forms are Jackie, Jackee, Jacquine, Jacotte, Jacquenetta, Jaclyn, and there are probably others.

Jessica *(Hebrew) "Wealth"*

This is another name that has the sound of coins clinking in the background, to the delight of Taurus, Capricorn, and Leo. Some people make Jess and Jessie nickname forms, while others feel these are a separate name.

Judith *(Hebrew) "Praised"*

Capricorn and Virgo are frequently praised for their efforts, though never quite as much as they feel they deserve. Judy and Jody are short forms, Judy being particularly prone to humor as a result of being paired with Punch all these years. Jodie is sometimes given to boys as well as girls.

Julia *(Latin) "Youth"*

Gemini, Virgo, and Capricorn are the youthful signs of the Zodiac. Variant forms abound, because this was a highly popular name a few years ago; it seems to be falling back these days. Some of the variants are Julie, Juliet, Juliana, Julienne, Giulia, Jill, Jillian, and Gillian.

Matsu *(Japanese) "Pine"*

The Japanese consider the pine the tree of January, which certainly makes sense to me. The rest of the year, evergreens get lost among the other trees, but in winter they stand out. Some people spell this Matsue.

Mehitable *(Hebrew) "Whom the Lord benefits"*

You can give this to Aquarius in recognition of her good fortune, but why not try it on Capricorn, as an antidote? There seem to be hundreds of ways to spell this name: Mehetabel, Mehitabel, Metabel, and so on. Hitty and Metty are the nickname forms.

CAPRICORN

Melanie *(Greek/French)* *"Black"*

Black is one of Capricorn's traditional colors. Variants are Melina, Melinda, Mel, Melan, Melly, and Melony. I can't see any good coming from naming a girl Melony.

Narcissus *(Greek)* *"Daffodil"*

The daffodil, or narcissus, is the plant for December, so the name can be given to Capricorn or Sagittarius. You might also give a thought to narcissism, excessive self-worship, and give it to a Leo. it has been given as a boy's name, too. Variant forms are Narcisse, Narcissa, and, of course, Daffodil.

Natalie *(French)* *"Christmas child"*

A Christmas child is going to come up a Capricorn, obviously. Variants are Natalia, Netty, Natasha, and Tasha. Natasha doesn't mean Christmas as much these days; it tends to refer to a seething, sensuous foreign spy. So perhaps it would do well on a Scorpio. A Capricorn could also be a seething, sensuous foreign spy, provided that fit in with her career goals. Spelled Nathalie (but pronounced Natalie), it is sometimes used as a feminine form of Nathaniel.

Paige *(French)* *"Attendant, page"*

Unless you live in a palace, the pages you are most likely to see today (disregarding the pages of this book) are the people who work in libraries, running to the shelves to get books for people. People who called out to people in hotel lobbies about messages used to be called pages, but now we seem to be inclined to call them pagers. At any rate, pages are people who do a lot of work, industrious people (except when they're fetching a book I've asked for). This should go to Capricorn or Virgo. Boys have also been named Paige, or Page.

Priscilla *(Latin)* *"From ancient times"*

Cancer and Capricorn are the signs most attuned to history and tradition. There used to be a magazine called *Modern Priscilla*; I don't recall just what they were trying to prove. The pet form is Prissy, which you could give to a Virgo, but don't. Just don't, that's all. Cilla is an acceptable substitute.

CAPRICORN

Shannon *(Irish) "Small, wise, old one"*

Capricorn is long-lived, and inclined to become a company equivalent of the tribal elder of olden days. The Celtic names starting with sh have been wildly popular for the last decade or so, and Shannon has been riding the same wave, being given to both boys and girls.

Simone *(Hebrew) "Heard"*

The onomasts are in favor of saying that Simon means "One who hears" but Simone means "one who is heard." I don't know if this is a linguistic quibble, or if the onomasts are making a sexist joke. Maybe I just missed something somewhere. Capricorn is a sign that will both listen and be heard; I'm taking no chances. The name is sometimes pronounced with two syllables, and sometimes with three.

Sophia *(Greek) "Wisdom"*

All the signs have some form of wisdom; Capricorn and Cancer are most likely to draw theirs from tradition and experience. Variant forms include Sofia and Zofia, as well as Sonja, which comes in a variety of bizarre spellings, from Sonia and Sonya to Zoneea and the sky's the limit. I heard of someone who was thinking of naming her twins Sonea and Yetsofa. I think she was joking.

Zinita *(Hebrew) "God's gracious gift"*

See John, under Aries boys, and Jane, under Virgo girls, for notes on these kinds of names. I don't know about where you live, but where I come from there was an unexplained run of Zinitas around the turn of the century. One of them, Zinita B. Graf, went on to become an actress of fair-to-middling popularity. The phenomenon was recorded for all time in Zaneeta Shinn, a turn-of-the-century Iowa girl in Meredith Willson's "The Music Man."

CAPRICORN
BOYS' NAMES

Broderick *(Welsh)* *"Son of Roderick" or "Son of a hero"*

Some people don't like to be known as the child of someone else; they insist on their own, separate identities. Capricorn, Cancer, Libra, and Pisces are less likely to be picky about this than the other signs. Brod and Broddy are pet forms.

Clark *(English)* *"One who is literate"*

This generally implied a scholar or a clergyman. (In fact, this is where the words clerk and clergy came from.) Cancer and Capricorn are the most likely to spend their time studying old things.

Craig *(Celtic)* *"Crag"*

Scorpio and Capricorn are most likely to appreciate the gloomy atmosphere of a cold stone peak.

Damien *(Greek)* *"Taming"*

These are the people who want power, not to be on top and get applause or money, but so they can be sure that everything is run "right." Virgo, Scorpio, Taurus, and Capricorn are this sort. Damen and Damian are variants.

Darcy *(Gaelic)* *"Dark"*

Most of Capricorn's colors are dark, and the shortest day of the year comes at the beginning of his month. The name, also spelled Darce and D'Arcy, is frequently given to girls, too.

Eldon *(German)* *"Respected elder"*

Capricorn respects his elders and, with his life expectancy and dignity, aspires to be a respected elder in his turn. Elton, Alden, and Aldon are variants.

CAPRICORN

Emil *(German)* *"Diligent"*

Capricorn and Virgo are industrious and thorough. The name is also spelled Emile and Emilio. Emily is a feminine form.

Emmett *(German)* *"Industrious"*

This is also related to the Anglo-Saxon word meaning "ant," another insect that is always held up to us as a good example. (Where do all these people who want us to act like bugs come from? Under a rock?) Virgo and Capricorn are the workaholics of the Zodiac.

Enoch *(Hebrew)* *"Educated, dedicated"*

This sounds like something for Virgo and Capricorn, who are certainly dedicated, and are frequently educated. About once every generation, the mystics bring up the matter of the Book of Enoch, an apocalyptic work written thousands of years ago, but left out of the Bible because church authorities couldn't see much use to it. The name Enoch becomes fashionable again for a few years, and then the fuss dies down again until next time.

Giles *(Greek)* *"Young goat"*

This is sometimes considered a form of Julius, and people who pronounce it with a soft G are showing that influence. Other people say it with a hard G. In its goat reference, it makes a fine name for Capricorn, and, I think, for any kid. (Sorry.)

Henry *(German)* *"Ruler of the home"*

Virgo, Leo, Scorpio, and Capricorn are frequently domestic masters, sometimes tyrants. Henry has been very popular over the years, and there are plenty of variant forms: Enrico, Enrique, Henri, Heinz, Heinrich, Heinie, Hank, Harry, Hal, Hendrik, and Henryk are a few. Henry seems to be out of style at the moment, but it's one of those names that always comes back.

Ichabod *(Hebrew)* *"Glory has departed"*

This is a gloomy name for gloomy sorts like Scorpio or Capricorn. It is also spelled Icabod. I have heard of children nicknamed Icky, but I believe that was an editorial comment rather than an abbreviation of their name.

CAPRICORN

Immanuel *(Hebrew) "God is with us"*

This is a traditional Christmas name, as well as an optimistic note to cheer up Capricorn's gloomier hours. Manuel and Emmanuel are variants.

Ishmael *(Arabic/Hebrew) "God will hear"*

Like the preceding name, this is an optimistic pronouncement. You may give it to the more optimistic signs, Leo, Gemini, and Sagittarius, or use it to try to cheer up the pessimistic ones, Capricorn, Scorpio, and Cancer.

James *(Hebrew) "Supplanter"*

This is one of the most popular variants of Jacob, and has had a large following throughout history. More presidents of the United States have been named James than any other first name. Why, there was even one who was known as Jimmy. Virgo, Scorpio, and Capricorn are the supplanters of the Zodiac, people who will forge ahead and get the boss's job. Other forms of the name are Jim, Jimmy, Jamie, Jaime, and Hamish. Jamie is often used as a feminine form.

Jordan *(Hebrew) "To descend"*

The onomasts feel this implies a child, a descendant. Capricorn, Cancer, Pisces, and Libra are most likely to be proud of their parents. It is a river name, and like many river names is given to both boys and girls, though some people prefer Jordana as a feminine form.

Lambert *(German) "Land bright"*

Capricorn and Cancer are the most inclined to be patriotic, to consider their land bright. You want to be careful about using this; no matter how much you call him Bert, someone's going to call him Lamb. Lambrecht is a variant, but that doesn't solve much.

Linus *(Greek) "Flaxen-haired"*

Yes, but the name is most famous as the intellectual with the security blanket, in "Peanuts." This sounds like Cancer and Capricorn.

CAPRICORN

Matthew *(Hebrew)* *"Gift of God"*

See John, under Aries boys, for comments on these "gift" names. Matt, Mateo, and Matthias are some variants.

Noel *(French)* *"Christmas"*

Christmas children have much to bear. I know a woman who intended to name her Christmas child Exma. (From Xmas, see?) No one could argue her out of it except the stubborn baby herself, who insisted on being born on December 24. The child was named Chloe Zoe instead, because whe was born so "chloze" to Christmas. She throws blocks in her daycare center, and I don't blame her. Noelle is a feminine variant; Nuell is sometimes used for boys.

Oren *(Hebrew)* *"Pine"*

The experts argue a lot about just what kind of tree it was, exactly, that the Israelites called Oren. Some insist it was a fir, while others claim there aren't any firs growing in the Middle East so how could have anyone have needed a word for fir? Fortunately, this hardly matters here. As mentioned under Matsu, in Capricorn girls, this is the season for evergreen trees, from now through Pisces. Capricorn, particularly, is well represented by an evergreen because Capricorns stay youthful-looking. Oran, Orin, and Orrin are variants.

Otto *(German)* *"Prosperous"*

Is this some odd masculine version of Ada? I don't recall any of the onomasts pointing this out, particularly, but it sounds like a possibility. Anyway, as previously noted, Taurus, Capricorn, and Leo are the prosperous members of the Zodiac.

Ryan *(Gaelic)* *"Prince"*

Leo, Aries, and Scorpio are the king types of the Zodiac. Capricorn and Virgo are the sort to belong in the next level down, the people who are right up near the top without actually being at the peak.

CAPRICORN

Scott *(English) "Scotsman"*

Prosperous signs known for their frugality and "prudent self-interest" are Taurus and Capricorn. I suppose this will get me in trouble, being just short of an ethnic joke. But the only gung-ho Scotsman I know wears a button on St. Andrew's Day that says "Kiss Me, I'm Scottish. 50¢ a Kiss." When he sees this, he will write me an indignant letter. It will arrive postage due. To appease him, perhaps, I will add the observation that people from Scotland are Scots, or Scottish. Scotch is a term properly applied only to whiskey, broth, tape, and terriers.

Sebastian *(Greek) "Venerable, revered"*

Capricorn is long-lived and insists on respect. Some people spell this Sebastien.

Stanley *(English) "Stony field"*

Life is like that to a Capricorn or a Scorpio. Stan is the commonest nickname, though some people prefer Stosh.

Timothy *(Greek) "Honoring God"*

Cancer, Capricorn, Taurus, and Scorpio, in sometimes wildly varying ways, are honorers of God. In the case of Capricorn, convictions will be reinforced by a feeling that religious devotion represents a traditional value. Tim and Timmy are the pet forms of the name. Other variants are Timoteo, Timothee, and Timotheus. Some people will name girls Timothea or Timmie.

Ulrich *(German) "Noble ruler"*

Aries, Leo, and Scorpio have the most inclination this way, but, as noted under Ryan and elsewhere, Capricorn and Virgo have a definite bent in that direction as well. A variant is Alaric.

William *(German) "Helmet of resolution"*

When I was a child, I used to read name books that told some story about a legendary helmet of willpower. For some reason, I have not seen the story since. Have onomasts given up on it, or was the author of that child's

CAPRICORN

name book just putting me on? At any rate, Scorpio, Aries, Virgo, Capricorn, and Taurus are the most self-willed of signs. There are plenty of variant forms and nicknames, including Wil, Will, Willie, Willy, Bill, Billy, Willis, Guillaume, Guglielmo, Wilhelm, and Willem.

AQUARIUS

the Water-Bearer

January 22 to February 21

I checked one of those astrological guides to this and that, and found a chart of colors that are appropriate to every sign: red for Aries, black for Capricorn, and so on. Under Aquarius, it said, "Paisleys and plaids."

That about sums it up. Aquarius has always been the most psychedelic of signs: brilliant, creative, and a bit out of synch. Aquarians are the life of the party. They love challenges, puzzles, and making new friends. Anything new and original and liberated is their lifeblood.

They are also impractical, unpredictable, and contrary. Utterly unimpressed by authority or tradition, they are the rebels, the trend-setters. They are even-tempered, though. Injustice or restriction of freedom may make them mad, but never so mad they can't think of something to do about it. They won't throw a tantrum or blow off steam; they'll act.

Aquarius is just a whirlwind. It is also considered the luckiest sign of the Zodiac.

Semi-famous Aquarians include Lloyd Alexander, Gelett Burgess, Jules Feiffer, Frank Frazetta, Johnny Hart, George MacManus, C. L. Moore, Ronald A. Knox, Mary Lasswell, Sax Rohmer, Louis Slobodkin, and Gahan Wilson.

AQUARIUS
GIRLS' NAMES

Andrea *(Latin) "Manly"*

Or is it? See Cheryl, under Leo girls, and Andrew, in this section. Andra, Andrina, Drena, and Rena are variants.

Barbara *(Greek) "Stranger, outlandish one"*

Aquarius and Gemini are always considered a little strange by less progressive signs. I don't know how much it matters to you that this word, which comes from the same roots as the word "barbarian," originally meant "Those guys over there with the beards." But, if you really want to go into it, Aquarius is considered the most androgynous of signs, and perhaps a bearded woman fits in. But enough of that; variants of the name include Barb, Barbie, Barbi, Babette, Babs, Bobbi, Bonny, Babe, Varina, and Basha.

Belinda *(Norse/Italian) "Beautiful snake"*

The beautiful snake, I am told, was a symbol of wisdom and immortality. This is the sort of arcane symbolism that would amuse Aquarius and Pisces.

The onomasts always get excited over this mystic snake, which turns up in any name with a "lind" in it. They do not know why the Norse and Italians should get together on the beautiful snake, and have a fine time trying to think of other ways out. Some said it was simply a cross between bella and linda, which would have meant "pretty pretty." But that would have left the snake out, so it would never do. Others tried to trace it to some other kind of snake, and are no doubt working on the implication of Baal worship in Norse names. If you hear what they decide before I do, let me know.

Cassandra *(Greek) "Helper of men"*

This is really just another form of Alexander, but that's too easy for the onomasts, who want to allude somehow to the original Cassandra, a prophetess who was cursed by Apollo (Apollo had a tendency to do this to young ladies who just said no) to be always right but never believed. The name has a touch of ill omen about it, and might do better for Scorpio or Capricorn, though Aquarius is handy at both prophecy and helping mankind. You choose. Cass, Cassie, Sassy, Sandy, Sandra, and Casey are nickname forms.

Celia *(Latin) "Heavenly"*

This seems to specifically refer to the sky, and ought to go to one of the air signs, Gemini, Libra, or Aquarius. Celine, Celeste, Celestine, and Celina are variants. Some people add Cecilia.

Colette *(Greek) "Victory of the people"*

Most onomasts agree this is a form of Nicholas, by way of Nicolette, though there are a few who try to make it out to be a form of the French word for necklace. Aquarius is the type to strive toward a people's victory. Nichole, Nicola, and Nicoline are variants. (There are babies who have been named Nicotine, too, but that's probably beside the point.)

Dixie *(American) "South"*

Some people have made a life's work out of trying to figure out why the South is called Dixie. Is it because of the Mason-Dixon line? Is it derived from the French word for ten? Is it from the Latin for "I have spoken"? Let the word scientists work on that. It is used as an informal, perky name, the sort Gemini, Aquarius, or Sagittarius would be happy with. There are going to be jokes about Dixie cups. Some people just have that kind of mind.

Gloria *(Latin) "Glorious"*

This is a name for the egotists of the Zodiac, Leo, Scorpio, and Aries. Still, the mystics have got us all looking for a new age, the Age of Aquarius, which is supposed to be glorious and filled with wonder. Why not anticipate a bit and give your Aquarius a glorious name? Variants include Gloriana and Glory.

Ida *(German) "Happy, prosperous"*

The shortest names give the onomasts the most trouble, and there was disagreement on this. But the majority seems to feel it's another form of

AQUARIUS

Ada. The prosperous signs are Leo, Taurus, and Capricorn, while the happy ones are Aquarius, Sagittarius, and Pisces. Short names also seem to bother parents, who have created such grand forms are Ideona, Idelle, and Ideena.

Letitia *(Latin) "Gladness"*

Sagittarius, Pisces, and Aquarius are cheerful signs. Leo and Gemini are signs, also inclined to be optimistic. Lettice and LaTisha are variants of this, while Lita, Leta, Letty, and Tish are pet forms.

Madeline *(Hebrew) "Tower"*

Aquarius and Leo are the taller of the signs of the Zodiac. A lot of onomasts disagree with this definition, feeling it is more of a tribute to Mary Magdalene. (in this case, Magdalene means "A woman from Magdala.") The name has also given birth to the word magdalene, meaning a woman of ill repute, and maudlin, sloppily sentimental. The pronunciation is no easier; at various times, the name has been pronounced to rhyme with line, lane, and lean. Variants include Magdalene, Madeleine, Magda, Maga, Maeli, Malen, and Mado. Maddy is the nickname form.

Mercedes *(Spanish) "Mercies"*

This is another title of the Virgin Mary that became a name. Libra, Sagittarius, Pisces, and Aquarius tend to have mercy on others. If Mercedes makes you think of a car, give the name to Leo, Aries, or Scorpio. Mercy is also sometimes used as a name.

Nadine *(Slavic) "Hope"*

Leo and Sagittarius are the more optimistic and Aquarius also tends to look to the future with hope. Nadia and Nadezhda are variants.

Naomi *(Hebrew) "Pleasant"*

Aquarius and Libra are the most even-tempered of signs. I have no idea where the name Naomi has gone; you simply don't see it these days among all the Shaunas and Jordans and Jennifers. Naamah is a variant.

Ophelia *(Greek) "Immortality, wisdom"*

The more mystic of the onomasts say this is another reference to that mysterious snake, though "lind" does not appear in this name anywhere. It is thus another arcane name for those who are interested in such things: Aquarius and Pisces. Ophelie and Ofelia are variants.

Orchid *(English) "Orchid"*

This is an exotic and romantic flower, the sort of thing for Scorpio or Aquarius. Some people call just any corsage an orchid. Try to not let it get to you.

Pandora *(Greek) "Gifted"*

Aquarius is that, all right. The original Pandora was the first woman on earth, according to the Greeks. The gods invented her as a way of getting back at men. The Greek attitude toward women was always iffy, to say the least. Dora is a nickname form.

Pansy *(French) "Thought"*

Not only is Aquarius a deep thinker, but the pansy happens to be one of the flowers attributed to the sign. Applied to a woman, Pansy always seems to imply a fresh, freckled country girl. Applied to a man, it meant a wimp, and sounded a lot nastier, too.

Prudence *(English) "Prudence"*

Taurus is actually the most prudent, or cautious, of signs, but why not try this on a Gemini or Aquarius? It might tone them down a little, and every little bit helps. Pru and Prue are nickname forms.

Rowena *(Celtic) "White mane" or "Fair and slender"*

Aquarius is regarded as both slender and good-looking. I don't know what you can do about the white mane. Rhonwen is a variant.

Sharon *(Hebrew) "Plain"*

One onomast adds that the plain of Sharon was known for its exotic beauty and fertility. It sounds like the sort of place for an Aquarius. Some experts, however, say this is just another form of Sarah. Shari is used as a nickname for both, as is Sherry.

Shelby (Anglo-Saxon) "Farm on the ledge"

Aquarius and Gemini would both enjoy a life on the brink. This name is given to both boys and girls. Selby is a variant; Shel or Shelley is the nickname.

Shirley (Anglo-Saxon) "White meadow"

If you think the meadow is white because it is full of sun-ripened crops, give it to the harvest signs, say, Virgo and Libra. If you think it's white because it's covered with snow, give it to Capricorn, Aquarius, or Pisces. Shirley is sometimes used as a boy's name, too. Sherrill, a variant, is used for both sexes as well. Sherrey, Sherrie, Sher, and Cher are used as variants. (Cher is also considered a form of Cherry, Cheri, or even just Cher, which means "dear" or "expensive" in French.)

Tamara (Hebrew/Russian) "Palm tree"

I'm not sure why the Russians needed a word for palm tree, but there it is. The palm tree is a symbol of slenderness, grace, and beauty, all of which Aquarius has in abundance. Tamar, Tamour, and Tamah are variants, but by far the most popular form of the name is Tammy.

Venetia (Celtic) "Blessed"

The majority of the experts are agreed that this is a form of the Welsh name Gwyneth, and not, as others insist, a reference to people from Venice. Aquarius, by virtue of her good fortune, is considered blessed.

Vivian (Latin) "Lively"

The liveliest signs in the Zodiac are Gemini, Aquarius, Sagittarius, Leo, Aries, and Scorpio. Vivien and Vivienne are variants. Viv is the usual nickname.

Wanda (German) "Wanderer"

It's up to you to decide what this means. Pisces wanders a bit because she's never quite sure where she wants to go. Gemini, Aquarius, and

AQUARIUS

Sagittarius wander because they like to get around. Scorpio and Capricorn wander because they never feel at home anywhere. Variant forms are Vanda, Vonda, LaVonda, LaWanda, Wendy, and, believe it or not, Wendeline.

Zilpah *(Hebrew) "Sprinkling"*

In many parts of the country, it is said to be sprinkling when there is a very light, gentle rain falling. This is generally a refreshing kind of day, the sort of day epitomized by Gemini or Aquarius. Some people prefer to spell this name Zilpha.

Zoe *(Greek) "Life"*

As mentioned above, the lively signs are Gemini, Aquarius, Sagittarius, Leo, Aries, and Scorpio. Gemini and Aquarius could deal best with a Z for their first initial. The variants are even more exotic: Zoa, Zoelle, Zola, Zoey, Zooey, Zowie, and Zoya.

AQUARIUS
BOYS' NAMES

Aaron *(Hebrew) "Enlightened"*

If there is one adjective Aquarius would like to have attached to his name, this is the one. Some onomasts disagree with this meaning, some saying it means "high mountain" and some arguing that it isn't a Hebrew name at all, but an Egyptian one. I have a feeling this is an argument that will go on for a while; let's move along while they work on it. Aron is a variant spelling.

Albert *(German) "Noble, bright"*

You may use this as another aristocratic sign for Leo, Scorpio, and Aries, or you may take it symbolically as another name meaning enlightenment, in which case it belongs to Aquarius. Al and Bert are the common pet forms. Variants include Aubert, Albrecht, Adelbert, Adalbert, and Ethelbert.

AQUARIUS

Alexander *(Greek) "Defender and helper of men"*

Gemini and Aquarius would find that sort of role to their liking. If the name makes you think of Alexander the Great, however, you may prefer to give it to warlike Aries or Scorpio, despite all attempts made to give Alexander a reputation for humanitarian goals. It has been a popular name, either way. Feminine forms include Alexandra, Alexandrine, Alexis, Sasha, and Sandy. Male variants include Alastair, Alistair, Iskander, Sikander, Alessandro, Sandor, Sandro, Alexi, Alexis, Alex, Alec, Sandy, Saunder, and Al. Vaudeville Scotsmen were generally known as Sandy.

Alfred *(German) "Elf counselor"*

The name seems to imply someone getting advice from or giving advice to some supernatural beings. Gemini, Aquarius, and Pisces are likely to get caught up in an adventure like that. Alfred the Great is known as a progressive and humanitarian leader. Alf and Alfie are the nickname forms; Alfredo, Alfeo, and sometimes Avery are variants.

Algernon *(French) "With beard" or "With mustache"*

You'd think that would be an easy decision, but the name experts can't make up their minds. In any case, these are considered masculine ornaments, so the name should probably go to one of the masculine signs: Aries, Gemini, Leo, Libra, Sagittarius, or Aquarius. Algy, or Algie, is the nickname form.

Andrew *(Latin) "Manly"*

This would also seem to belong to the masculine signs listed above. Variants are Andre, Andreas, Ander, Drew, Anders, and Andy. The variant Andrea used to be a boy's name, but people decided it looked more like a girl's, with that a on the end, and it is now used almost solely as a feminine form.

Barry *(Irish) "Javelin"*

You may consider the javelin a weapon, for warlike Scorpio and Aries, as a piece of sporting equipment, for Sagittarius, or as an indication of the slimness of Aquarius.

AQUARIUS

Benedict *(Latin)* *"Blessed"*

You may give this to Aquarius in recognition of his luck, or to Capricorn, as an antidote for his. Variants are Benito, Benedetto, Benoit, and Bennett. Ben and Benny are the nickname forms.

Benjamin *(Hebrew)* *"Fortunate, strong"*

What this name literally means is "Son of the right hand," and is meant to imply everything that right-handed meant to the ancients: good fortune, dexterity, intelligence, expertise, and so on. I don't believe there are any names saluting the left hand. At any rate, Aquarius is dexterous and fortunate, though he is likely to be caught up in things like crusades for the rights of lefthanders. Ben, Benny, Benji, and Jamie are pet forms.

Bertram *(German)* *"Bright raven"*

The raven, as mentioned before, is one of those characters in folklore who seems to glory in throwing a monkey wrench into the works. (Okay, the people who created the folk tales hadn't heard of monkey wrenches, but I'm sure you get the point.) Aquarius and Sagittarius have touches of that, especially for a good cause, though Sagittarius will also do it just to be ornery. Bartram is a variant; Bert and Bertie are the pet forms.

Blaine *(Celtic)* *"Thin"*

Aquarius is one of the slimmer signs of the Zodiac. It is more common, perhaps, as a surname, or last name, but being short, it has been applied to heroes of paperback romances and will thus probably experience a wave of popularity.

Conrad *(German)* *"Bold, wise counselor"*

There are other signs more likely to give advice, but when Aquarius does give it, he will not err on the timid side. Leo and Gemini are also like this. Curt and Kurt are sometimes used as nickname forms.

Dexter *(Latin)* *"Dexterous"*

This name literally means right, as in right-handed, the opposite of left, which is sinister. We do not have room here to go into all the anti-left-hand atrocities of history, but you will check to see that the lad is right-handed before you name him Dexter, won't you?

Dietrich *(German) "People rule"*

This sounds like another one of those humanitarian causes so beloved of Aquarius. Didrick, Dieter, Dirk, Thierry, and Theodoric are variants.

Doran *(Greek) "Gift"*

See John, under Aries boys, for these "gift" names. Some onomasts disagree, making it (Celtic) "Stranger." Aquarius will frequently be considered an outsider, always coming up with foreign ideas and odd concepts, so the name can fit him either way.

Ezra *(Hebrew) "Help"*

Leo, Gemini, and Aquarius are likely to be first on the scene to give assistance. Like a lot of Biblical names which took root on the farms of the "Bible Belt," this one has taken on a sort of hayseed aura.

Felix *(Latin) "Fortunate, happy"*

Aquarius is both; you could also give the name to Sagittarius or Leo. The name is also related to the word feline, which is why there's a character named Felix the Cat.

Francis *(German) "Free man"*

Aquarius, Sagittarius, and Gemini value their personal freedom, sometimes above anything else. There are some onomasts who feel this simply means "Frenchman." Variants include Francisco, Franco, Frank, Francois, and Chico. Frances, Francoise, and Francine are some of the feminine versions.

Gustave *(German) "Staff of the gods"*

This sounds mystic and mysterious, the sort of thing Pisces and Aquarius would dote on. Gustaf is a variant; Gus is the obvious pet form.

AQUARIUS

Hamilton *(English)* *"Beautiful mountain"*

Gemini, Aquarius, Sagittarius, Aries, Leo, and Scorpio are your mountain climbers, but the first three are the ones most likely to do it for the view. Ham is the nickname form.

Herschel *(Yiddish)* *"Deer"*

We view deer as swift, graceful animals darting hither and yon in the forest. Sagittarius, Aquarius, and Gemini are the ones most likely to live up to the image. Hersh is the nickname form. Heshel and Herzl are variants.

Jason *(Greek)* *"Healer"*

Libra and Aquarius are often possessed with a desire to heal all the world's wounds. This name, long ignored, boomed suddenly during the last twenty years, in response to some popular demand that I must have slept through. The use of the name for the masked slasher of the movies has not diminished its popularity yet. There is no real nickname form, though Jayce is sometimes used.

Jerome *(Greek)* *"Mystic name"*

This is the sort of thing that Pisces and Aquarius would enjoy. Mysticism always interests the Aquarius, unless, of course, everyone else is doing mysticism this year, in which case it's old hat, and beneath his notice. Jerry is the nickname form. Variants include Gerome, Geronimo, and Hieronymus.

Neill *(Irish)* *"Champion"*

You have the same choice of definitions here as you did with Nigel. If champion means to you the winner, the fellow who came up with the gold medal, then Aries, Leo, and Scorpio are probably the ones who would suit the title best. But if you go with the old meaning of a person who champions a cause, who stands up for something, then Aquarius and Scorpio are the men for the name. Variants are Neil, Nel, Nils, and Nels.

Nicholas *(Greek)* *"Victory of people"*

This sounds like another cause that would be championed by Aquarius.

Variants include Claus, Colin, Nicolas, Nick, Nicky, Nikita, Nicol, and sometimes Nils. Nicola, Nicole, and Nicolette are feminine forms.

Omar *(Arabic) "Firstborn son"*

But most Omars are named for Omar, the firstborn son of Mohammed, who, after his father died, took the ball and ran with it, so to speak. Taking leadership of a new religion is the sort of thing Aquarius or Scorpio would do well. Other Omars are named for Omar Khayyam, the depressing hedonist poet, and Omar N. Bradley, the general. Omer is a variant.

Oscar *(English) "Divine spear"*

This sounds like Aquarius: long, thin, and mysterious. The onomasts do not go into much detail about whether this is supposed to be a reference to some specific divine spear (a spear dedicated to Odin, say, or the lance that pierced Christ's side) or whether it applies to divine spears in general. Nowadays, it's Oscar the Grouch, of "Sesame Street," a fine gentleman who lives in a garbage can. Variants are Oskar and Ozzie.

Sean *(Hebrew) "God'gracious gift"*

See John, under Aries boys, for notes on "gift" names. This is one of those Celtic Sh names that became very popular about the same time Jason came along. It is generally spelled the way it's pronounced, Shawn or Shaun, by those of us who don't have the Gaelic. Shauna, Shawna, and Seana are sometimes given to girls.

Wallace *(German) "Welshman"*

But originally, the word meant a stranger, a barbarian, one of bizarre and outlandish customs. (The Welsh weren't all that popular with their neighbors.) Aquarius will generally be, like the Welsh, about half a step more civilized than anyone else, and will be considered bizarre because of it. Wally and Walsh are variants. Wallis has been given to girls.

Webster *(Anglo-Saxon) "Weaver"*

This is a name for someone with dexterity and knowledge of his craft. It probably refers to an Aquarius or a Virgo. Web and Webb are short forms.

AQUARIUS

Xavier *(Spanish)* *"New house"*

Did you think this meant savior all along, the way I did? It really belongs to Aquarius, I suppose, the most progressive and thus, perhaps, the "newest" house of the Zodiac. It is not very often used except in tribute to St. Francis Xavier. There used to be a lot of Francis X. Rileys and such; this custom seems to be fading. The female form is Xaviera, but no one has exactly been rushing to use it since Xaviera Hollander brought out *The Happy Hooker*.

PISCES
the Fish
February 22 to March 21

Unless, as is likely, you skipped ahead to this sign instead of reading all the elegant prose that preceded it, you may recall that Aries came at the front of the Zodiac, and is considered one of the most single-minded, dynamic signs in the whole zoo. What do you think we may expect of the last sign, Pisces?

That's right. Pisces is known for being wishy-washy, weak-willed, unworldly, indecisive, vague, easily confused, unambitious, easily led, afraid of mice, and just generally the sum of everything that is meant in the phrase "poor fish."

On the bright side, if that's what you want to call it, Pisces is the most sensitive of the characters in the Zodiac. Pisces natives are sympathetic, sentimental, peaceful folk, the intellectual, creative, psychic, romantic dreamers. They will make more friends than they will money, but with their gifts, they can expect to go far, almost in spite of themselves.

Several experts suggest that these creative souls who are quickly bored and easily panicked are naturals for the nursing profession. I can't see it, but perhaps I'm not sensitive enough.

Semi-famous fish include Milt Caniff, Mary Chase, Ernest Bramah, August Derleth, Fontaine Fox Jr., Edward Gorey, Kenneth Grahame, Allen J. Hubin, Clark Kent, Ring Lardner, Norman Lindsay, Arthur Machen, Reginald Marsh, Phyllis McGinley, and Dr. Seuss.

PISCES
GIRLS' NAMES

Abigail *(Hebrew) "Father of joy"*

You might not expect to have trouble with a fine old name like Abigail, but there it is. The words for "father" and "joy" are jammed together, and you are left to guess what that means. Does it mean "father of joy"? "Source of joy"? "My father is joy"? "My father rejoices"? "I am my father's joy"? Most of the meanings imply that the bearer is a source of joy to someone. Libra, Leo, and Pisces are the folks most concerned with that idea. Various forms of the name are Abby, Abbie, Abbey, Abbe, Gail, Gayle, and Abbigale.

    At one time the name signified a female servant, and was actually used as a noun meaning a personal maid, for a while.

Anemone *(Greek) "Breath"*

This became the name of a flower that looked to someone to be so fragile that it might blow away with one breath. Some people still call the anemone the windflower. Virgo is frail, but the anemone is more of a spring flower, so I would suggest it for Pisces, which is almost as delicate. There are people to this day who insist on spelling this Anenome. I always look it up to make sure, myself, and if I have time I look it up again just to be sure the fellow who printed the first dictionary wasn't fooling.

Brittany *(Latin) "From England"*

Brittany is itself a place name of a little branch of France, which was settled by the English and called Little Britain by them. A diminutive name like this, particularly of a place known for its fish, obviously goes to Pisces. Britt is a short form, while Brett is the masculine form. The soap operas seem to have made this name wildly popular over the past decade.

Brooke *(English) "Brook"*

This obviously belongs to one of the water signs: Cancer, Scorpio, or Pisces. Variants include Brookes, Brook, and Brookie. If your last name is Trout, I would consider something else. Anything else.

PISCES

Christina *(Latin)* *"Christian"*

You could apply this to anyone, really, but I have listed it under Pisces in recognition of the traditional use of the fish as a Christian symbol.

The Christians and the astrologers have been at each other for years, swapping nasty names and accusations. Part of the problem seems to be that all the important planets and constellations are named for gods of Greece and Rome. But, barring the possibility that someone will come along and rename them all, there's not much that can be done about that. (And don't think some people haven't tried it.) And there seems to be some concern over whether this sort of fortune-telling may not lead one to more lurid pursuits, until one is dancing under the trees during the full moon. I'd have to say it all depends.

My own feeling is that you are not committing a mortal sin by reading your horoscope every day, or even by writing your own. It is possible that you could be doing something more useful, but that's none of my business.

Where was I? Oh, yes. Christine, Kirsten, Kristin, Christiana, and Chrystal are some of the variants of Christina. Some of the pet forms are Chris, Chrissy, Crissie, Christy, and Tina. Christian is the form for boys.

Clementine *(Latin)* *"Merciful"*

There's also an overtone of peacefulness; one of the opposites is inclement, as in stormy weather. Libra, Pisces, Cancer, and Taurus are the signs more inclined toward mercy. Clementina and Clementia are variants; Clemmie is the usual nickname. The song may be considered a stumbling block. Every now and then there is a relevance movement in education and people stop teaching children such songs, and then a folk-song movement comes along and puts them right back in the curriculum. And what's wrong with that? Any movement that favors putting "Halle-lujah, I'm a Bum" back into the schoolbooks can't be all bad.

Cordelia *(Celtic)* *"Jewel of the sea"*

This name ought to go to the water signs, I think: Cancer and Pisces. The pet form Delia has some popularity on its own, but Cordy is a matter of taste. Some boys are given the form Cordell, but most of these are named for statesman Cordell Hull.

PISCES

Crystal *(English) "Crystal"*

This seems to be the sort of name for Aquarius and Pisces. Aquarius sees things more crystal-clear than Pisces, but both are interested in looking into the future, as through a crystal ball. Some people prefer to spell this Chrystal. Chris is the obvious pet form.

Dimity *(English) "Dimity"*

This is a crisp fabric mostly used for women's clothes. But some poets, taking their cue from the "dim" part of the word, have adopted it as a synonym for twilight, the close of the day. Pisces is the close of the year just as dusk is the close of the day, and you can't exactly name a girl Dusk.

Edna *(Hebrew) "Pleasure, delight"*

This name seems to be drawn from the same source as the name of the garden Adam and Eve inhabited. In fact, Eden is regarded as a variant form of the name, and does have its following. Pisces, Leo, and Libra are eager to be sources of delight.

Emma *(German)*

Well, this is one of *those* names. The onomasts are split pretty well down the middle on this, one camp saying it means "universal" and the other feeling it means "The Big One, The Great Ancestress, Grandmother." A compromise camp feels both are right, and that we are onto some earth-shaking revelation, the discovery of some archetype of an enormous, primeval, all-embracing grandmother. The idea makes me shudder (you'd have to have known my grandmother). At any rate, because of the undercurrent of mysticism, and because Pisces would rather like the idea of being the universal, all-comforting grandmother, I have put this here. It would probably apply to Libra as well. Emmie and Emmy are the pet forms. Some people consider Emmelie, Irma, and Erma to be variants.

Fawn *(English) "Fawn"*

Fawns are sweet, gawky, timid things, which seems to suit Pisces pretty well. By March, the year is edging along toward spring, too, which is when fawns start to turn up. Fawna is a popular variant, and some people use Fauna, but we are getting close here to the Latin names Fauna and

Faunus, which gets us into anthropological considerations and the powers of nature. I really don't feel up to all that today.

Faye *(French) "Fairy"*

The term "fairy" has gone through various meanings, even if you're only thinking of the supernatural creature. The fairy experts are now leaning more toward considering them beings of power and wonder rather than the little critters that dance on lily-of-the-valley. At any rate, Pisces would like the connection. Faye and Fae are also believed by some people to be short forms of the name Faith. Another related name is Fayette, drawn from the Marquis de Lafayette, the French hero of the American Revolution. He was so popular that the United States government actually had to order people to stop naming their towns Lafayette, because they were confusing the postal service. So a lot of towns named Fayette sprang up, and people liked the name. You will still meet a few Fayettes to this day.

Gay *(French) "Merry"*

You never know. The time may come when it's safe to use this as a name again. At any rate, it should go to the jovial signs, Pisces and Sagittarius.

Genevieve *(French/Celtic) "White wave, white as sea foam"*

The water signs, Pisces, Cancer, and Scorpio, obviously draw this one. In the form of Jennifer, it is supposedly one of the most popular girl's names around. I don't know; I seem to be surrounded by Ashleys and Brittanys and Jordans and Shannons, to name but a few. There are plenty of variants, if you like the name but want something a little less common. There are Gina, Genoveva, Ginevra, Jenny, Guinevere, Gwynever, and Gwenhwyfar. In one of the oldest of the King Arthur tales, Gwenhwyfar had a sister named Gwenhwyfach. This is a little too uncommon.

Helga *(Scandinavian) "Holy"*

You may give this to Taurus, Cancer, Capricorn, or Scorpio if you think of this as a religious reference, or to Aquarius and Pisces, who go in search of less traditional holies. A variant is Olga, made popular by St. Olga, who introduced Christianity to Russia and once massacred an entire city because it had ticked her off.

PISCES

Ina

The onomasts don't think much of Ina, particularly. They feel it's a pet name of something, but they haven't decided what yet. It may be a form of Agnes, or of Katherine, or of any name ending in "ine," or of just any Latin name. At any rate, it would probably do for someone who doesn't mind having a diminutive for a name, say, a Libra or a Pisces. It is usually pronounced as it's spelled, but it can also be pronounced ee-na, in which case, the onomasts note, it is the Japanese word for "now." I don't know how useful *that* bit of trivia is, but I am passing it along anyway.

Ingrid *(Scandinavian)* *"Hero's daughter"*

This is obviously between you and your ego. Capricorn, Cancer, Pisces and Taurus are most likely to be proud of their parents. Inga and Ingeborg are variants.

Joan *(Hebrew)* *"God's gracious gift"*

See John, under Aries boys, and Jane, under Virgo girls, for details. Some people consider this a version of Joanne, and pronounce it accordingly. Some people consider Joanne and Joanna to be forms of Joan, rather than abbreviations of Josephine Anne. I'm going to stay out of it, myself.

Leslie *(Celtic)* *"Grey fort"*

This is a kind of place for the more timid signs, Libra, Pisces, and Cancer, to take shelter. You might give it to Virgo because of the color. It is given to both boys and girls. Some onomasts claim it is just another form of Elizabeth. It is *not*.

Misty *(English)* *"Misty"*

Pisces, and perhaps Cancer, spends much of her life lost in a fog. Missy is sometimes considered a pet form.

Muriel *(Greek)* *"Myrrh, perfume"* *(Irish)* *"Sea-bright"*

The onomasts can't quite make up their minds, and the implication is that these were once two different names that kind of merged as the Irish-speaking people got acquainted with the Greek-speaking ones. As "sea-bright" it can go to one of the water signs, Cancer, Scorpio, and Pisces, while perfume is probably the concern of Pisces or Libra. Meriel is considered a form of this, and some people include Meryl and Myra. I have seen Miriel, but I suspect it's not a form of anything, since she had older sisters named Mariel and Muriel. Her parents may just have been naturally inventive.

Myrna (Gaelic) "Beloved, tender, gentle, polite, sweet, etc., etc., etc."

The gentle, darling signs are Libra and Pisces, and sometimes Cancer. Morna is considered a variant.

Peony (English) "Peony"

The peony is a flower long believed to have healing qualities, particularly valuable for women in labor. Isn't this a nice place to put it, nine months after the traditional month for weddings? How cheerful! How naive! How like Pisces!

Rachel (Hebrew) "Ewe"

A ewe is a female sheep, and everyone seems to agree that it is a symbol of gentle innocence, naiveté. That would make it a fine name for a Pisces.

But down in farm country, the word is that ewes are considered to be among the most vile-tempered, villainous creatures on earth. In some parts of the world, "ewe" is used as a substitute for "bitch" as an epithet. (The word "bitch" isn't what it used to be, either, but that doesn't really come within the scope of this collection.) So, depending on what you think of ewes, you might want to transfer it to Scorpio or Aries.

Variants include Raquel, Rae, Shelly, and Rachelle. Some people include Rochelle, too, though it is really a separate name.

Sybil (Greek) "Prophetess"

Aquarius and Pisces would be fascinated by sibyls and their works. Variants include Cybill, Sibyl, Sybylle, and Sibby. No one has told me whether the goddess Cybele is involved.

Tanya *(Slavic)* *"Fairy queen"*

This sounds like a job Pisces would enjoy. Tania, Tatiana, and Tawnia are variants. Some people consider Tawny the nickname form.

Thea *(Greek)* *"Divine"*

This is obviously another glory name for Leo, Aries, and Scorpio. But why not give mousy little Pisces a break? Variants are Theia and Teac.

Thelma *(Greek)* *"Nursling"*

I assume this means a child who is nursing, and not a baby nurse. Pisces, Libra, and Cancer are the most dependent signs. Thel is the usual nickname. Thelma is sometimes spelled, and pronounced, without the h.

Victoria *(Latin)* *"Victorious"*

This is another conquest name for Scorpio, Leo, and Aries. As the name of an era, however, it has come to symbolize, rightly or wrongly, a period when little girls led sheltered, quiet lives, got married, and lived quietly ever after. This is the sort of thing a Pisces would admire. Victoire is a variant; Vic and Vicky are nicknames.

Violet *(Latin)* *"Violet"*

This flower is a symbol of modesty and shyness, and is well suited for Pisces. It is also considered the traditional flower of February, which also makes it a Pisces or Aquarius name.

Just to confuse things, though, the violet is also considered the traditional flower of Taurus, and it serves as a symbol for the Bonaparte family, too. Use your own judgment.

Variants include Violette, Violaire, Violetta, Letta, Lola, Vi, Lolandi, Yolanda, and Iolanthe.

PISCES
BOYS' NAMES

Alan *(Gaelic)* *"Handsome, cheerful"*

Pisces is a jovial sign, and is good-looking as well. The name would also suit Libra. Variants include Allen, Alain, Allan, and Allyn.

Barnabas *(Hebrew)* *"Son of prophecy of consolation"*

Pisces people are always interested in prophecy, and generally need consolation, too. A prophecy of consolation is right up their alley. Barney is the nickname form. Onomasts disagree on whether Barnaby is a form of Barnabas, or a separate name, from the Aramaic word for "speech."

Chico *(Spanish)* *"Small"*

This is obviously a diminutive name. Some onomasts insist it is really a pet name for Francisco, while others say it is a pet name for Charles. At any rate, it does seem to indicate something small, and is probably suited to Pisces and Libra. Virgo's interest in little details might make this a good name for him, as well.

Claude *(Latin)* *"Lame, delicate"*

This is a name for the hesitant or the unlucky: Cancer, Capricorn, and Pisces. It may also be applied to Virgo, who has delicate health, or at least thinks he has. Claudius is a grandiose variant.

Curtis *(French)* *"Courteous"*

Libra and Pisces are courteous because it's nice; Virgo is courteous because it's the thing to do. Curt and Kurt are short forms.

Daryl *(Anglo-Saxon)* *"Well beloved"*

This is the sort of name that will reassure an insecure Pisces or Cancer. Darrell is a variant. In some parts of the country, both these names are pronounced "darl," which makes its relation to Darla and darling obvious.

Dean *(Anglo-Saxon) "Valley"*

This is one of those peaceful, protected places that Cancer, Libra, and Pisces like to think they'll retire to some day. Valleys are actually no more peaceful than mountains or prairies, but there's just something about the word. Deanie seems to have some currency as a feminine form.

Dewey *(Welsh) "Prized"*

Here is another chance to reassure Pisces and Cancer about what you think of them. This is actually a form of David, often grouped with Huey and Louie.

Erling *(Anglo-Saxon) "Nobleman's son"*

An earl's son, don't you see? This is another name that is really a tribute to the parents, rather than a salute to the child. Pisces, Cancer, Capricorn, and Taurus are likely to be proud of their parents.

Ervin *(Anglo-Saxon) "Sea friend"*

This ought to go to one of the water signs: Cancer, Scorpio, or Pisces. Irvin, Irving, Erv, and Irv are variants. Some onomasts are still arguing about whether Irwin and Erwin belong in the same group.

Florian *(Latin) "Flowering"*

This should go to the spring signs, Aries or Taurus. But Pisces is close, and spring might come early this year. Florent, Florenz, Florence, and Florentine are variants.

Gabriel *(Hebrew) "God is my strength"*

You could give this to anyone, but it might be the most help to those who are insecure about their own strength: Cancer, Pisces, or Libra. Gavril and Gabel are variants. Feminine forms are Gabrielle and Gabriella. Gabe seems to be the most common nickname form.

PISCES

Glen *(Gaelic) "Valley"*

In fact, the word glen is still used to mean a valley. This is another reference to a quiet, peaceful place for Cancer, Libra, or Pisces. It is sometimes spelled Glenn. Some people will use it for girls. You'd think, with all these names meaning valley, that the word valley itself might have become a name. This has not happened, though. (All those Vals you meet are Valeries, with the exception of Prince Valiant, of course.)

Grover *(Anglo-Saxon) "Grove"*

For some reason, when a forest becomes a "grove," people get all mystical and mysterious about it. They stop talking about "that there thicket" and start saying "yon grove." I don't know what the power is, but it's the sort of thing Aquarius and Pisces would enjoy.

Holden *(German) "Gentle, kind"*

Taurus, Cancer, Libra, and Pisces are the gentler signs of the Zodiac. Any blond named Holden will be known as Golden Holden as he grows up.

Hugh *(German) "Heart, mind"*

Pisces has both of these. They occasionally get in the way of each other. Hugo and Huey are variants, while Hughie is the pet form.

Isaac *(Hebrew) "Laughter"*

This should go to one of the jovial, sunny signs, like Leo, Pisces, and Sagittarius. Ike and Ikey are nicknames; the latter is in disrepute just now, from its days as an ethnic slur in vaudeville.

Kenneth *(Celtic) "Handsome"*

The good-looking signs (Libra, Scorpio, Pisces, and sometimes Sagittarius) snaffle this one. Ken and Kenny are the nickname forms. Some Celtophiles try all sorts of other spellings, from Kyneth to Cunedd. Kenna has been used as a feminine form.

Lyndon *(German) "Linden hill"*

I was expecting a fight on this one, because "lind," that syllable referring to mystic snakes, was in here, and onomasts love to argue about mystic snakes. But it seems this has meant linden trees for centuries, and the word for linden tree comes from an ancient word meaning linden tree. So this name is pretty secure in its meaning. Linden wood is very soft, very pliable, very useful. Libra and Pisces fit the description very well. Some people use Lindy as a nickname for this.

Magnus *(Latin) "Great"*

This is best applied to Leo, Aries, and Scorpio, with an occasional sop to Aquarius. But why not encourage that Pisces? He may grow into his name. Some people have been using Magnum as a variant; such people watch too much television. Apparently the name Magnolia is not related.

Marvin *(German) "Friend of the sea"*

Ervin, Irving, and Irwin all seem to be related to this somehow. Like them, it should go to one of the water signs: Scorpio, Cancer, or Pisces. Merwin is a variant spelling. Marv is the nickname form.

Maxwell *(Anglo-Saxon) "From the rich man's well"*

Here is another reference to water, for Cancer, Scorpio, and Pisces. I don't believe it would fit a Scorpio; he wouldn't care to be beholden to any rich man for his water. Max and Maxie are the nickname forms.

Monroe *(Celtic) "Red marsh"*

You may give this to Aries, for its color, or to the water signs, Cancer, Pisces, and Scorpio, for the moisture. Munro is a variant. Please don't ask me why Scorpio, the scorpion, is a water sign while Capricorn, the sea goat, and Aquarius, the water bearer, are not. That is not my department.

Murray *(Celtic) "Seaman"*

The water signs get this name, too, so apply it to Pisces, Cancer, or Scorpio. I will add that some modern astrologers feel that Pisces is really ruled, not by Jupiter, but by the planet Neptune, named for the Roman god of the sea. The ancients couldn't think of things like that because they hadn't heard about the planet Neptune.

Pasquale *(French) "Easter"*

Pisces or Aries can take this one. Pascal is another form of the name, sometimes used in honor of Blaise Pascal, the gentleman who came out with that famous dictum "I think, therefore I am." Sometimes I think I see a loophole in that, and sometimes I feel he has the right idea. It's related to Berkeleianism, I think: would you really be there if you weren't there to notice you were there? This is the sort of thing philosophers can bat around for hours, worrying about whether things are there or whether we just think they're there. This kind of nervousness belongs to Pisces and Cancer.

Paul *(Latin) "Small"*

I expected a name this widespread to require a little more set-up, but there it is. Libra and Pisces are interested in small things, while other signs have their eyes set on greatness. Variants include Paolo, Poul, Pol, Pablo, Pavel, and sometimes Apollo.

Perry *(French) "Pear tree"*

It's been a while since fruit trees were held up to us as good examples, but they're bringing back the concept. A fruit tree, you see, is supposed to be the model of the person who lives for others, producing good things that will nourish and nurture life. It's the kind of thing Libra and Pisces could get into. Personally, I don't believe the pear tree cares all that much, one way or the other, whether we have Pears á la Bordelaise or not.

Philip *(Greek) "Fond of horses"*

The use of this name depends on your perception of horses. If you see cart horses and plow horses, perhaps you'd better give it to Capricorn, Virgo, or Taurus. If you see wild stallions running across the plains, perhaps Scorpio is your man. If you see warriors on horseback, try Aries. Cowboys or adventurers on horses suggest Sagittarius. On the theory that Pisces is ruled by Neptune, though, it could go here. Neptune was regarded by the Greeks as the inventor of horses, and some of them suggested his relationship was even closer than that. There is such a thing as being too fond of horses. Phillip, Phillipe, and Felipe are some of the variant forms. Phil, Pippin, and Pip are used as nicknames. Phillippa is used as a feminine form, though some people pronounce it Phillip, just like the masculine form.

Samuel *(Hebrew) "Name of God"*

Gemini, Aquarius, and Pisces are the most likely people to be interested in the name of God, a rather arcane consideration. In most cultures, the name of God is something you keep quiet about, but there are always inquiring minds who want to know. Sam, Sammy, Sam'l, and Sammiwell are variants. Samson is considered a form of it by some. J. R. R. Tolkien gave us the form Samwise. The onomasts I consulted said the proper feminine form is Samuela, not Samantha.

Thaddeus *(Hebrew) "Praised"*

This is another name to reassure those delicate egos of Cancer and Pisces. Tadeusz is a variant. Tad and Thad are nicknames. (Tad is also a word for a small child, like tot; both tot and tad are also used as words for a small amount of something.)